Visitor's Guide
FRANCE:
CHAMPAGNE & ALSACE-LORRAINE

See page 190 for details of the
MPC *Visitor's Guides* to France.

D1561578

CHAMPAGNE & ALSACE-LORRAINE

BELGIUM

LUXEMBOURG

GERMANY

Givet

Rocroi
Renwez

Charleville-
Mézières   Sedan

Rethel   Montmédy   Longwy

ARDENNES

Thionville

Étain

Reims   Verdun   Metz

MARNE   Valmy   MOSELLE   Hunspach

Épernay   MEUSE   Haguenau

Châlons-
sur-Marne   Pont-à-
Mousson   Sarrebourg   Strasbourg

Montmirail   Bar-le-
Duc

Vitry-le-
François   Commercy   Toul   Nancy

MEURTHE-
ET-MOSELLE   Lunéville   BAS-
RHIN

St-Dizier   Baccarat

Brienne-le-
Château   Wassy   Mirecourt   St-Dié   Sélestat

Neufchâteau   HAUTE
MARNE   VOSGES   Ribeauvillé

Troyes   Piney   Vittel   Épinal

Bar-sur-Aube   Gérardmer   Colmar

AUBE   Chaumont   HAUT-
RHIN

Langres   Mulhouse

    Auberive   0   60km   Altkirch

0   40 miles

CHAPTER 1 Champagne-Ardenne

CHAPTER 2 Lorraine-Vosges

CHAPTER 3 Alsace

VISITOR'S GUIDE

FRANCE:
CHAMPAGNE &
ALSACE-LORRAINE

Barbara Mandell

MPC

Published by:
Moorland Publishing Co Ltd,
Moor Farm Road West, Ashbourne,
Derbyshire DE6 1HD England

ISBN 0 86190 517 2

British Library Cataloguing in Publication Data:
A catalogue record for this book is available from the British Library.

Colour origination by: DP Graphics, Wiltshire

Printed in Hong Kong by: Wing King Tong Co Ltd

Cover photograph: Colmar *(International Photobank)*
Rear cover: L' Épine *(B. Mandell)*
Page 3: Stork nest, Alsace area *(T. Oliver)*

The illustrations have been supplied by:
Tony Astle pp22, 59, 78, 94, 126, 142; Tony Oliver pp10, 102; MPC pp7
All the remainder by Barbara Mandell

MPC Production Team:
Editorial: Tonya Monk
Editorial Assistant: Christine Haines
Design: Ashley Emery
Cartography: Alastair Morrison

CONTENTS

Key to Symbols Used in Text Margin and on Maps

⛪	Church	🎿	Winter Sports
🏰	Castle	✳	Other Place of Interest
⊞	Building of Interest	🌸	Garden
🏛	Museum/Art Gallery	🌷	Beautiful View/Natural Phenomenon
🦙	Nature Reserve	🌳	Park
🇹	Archaeological Site	🦇	Cave
🚶	Walking	⛵	Water Sports

Key to Maps

▬▬▬	Motorway	⬙	City/Town
▬▬▬	Main Road	⬤	Town/Village
▭▭▭	Minor Road	∿	River/Lake
╌╌╌'	Province Boundary	╌╌╌:	National Boundary

How To Use This Guide

This MPC Visitor's Guide has been designed to be as easy to use as possible. Each chapter covers a region and gives all the background information to help you enjoy your visit. MPC's distinctive margin symbols, the important places printed in bold and a comprehensive index enable the reader to find the most interesting places to visit with ease.

At the end of each chapter an Additional Information section gives specific details such as addresses and opening times, making this guide a complete sightseeing companion.

At the back of the guide the Fact File, arranged in alphabetical order, gives practical information and useful tips to help you plan your holiday before you go and while you are there.

The maps of each region show the main towns, villages, roads and places of interest, but are not designed as route maps and motorists should always use a good recommended road atlas.

INTRODUCTION

The north-eastern corner of France is divided up into three different provinces, the most westerly being Champagne-Ardenne. Lorraine-Vosges is in the middle and, beyond it, Alsace is separated from Germany to the east by the River Rhine. It also has a very short frontier with Switzerland in the south-east, more or less on the outskirts of Basel. Lorraine-Vosges shares its northern border with Germany, Luxembourg and Belgium whereas Champagne-Ardenne's only foreign neighbour is Belgium to the north. In France itself the region is bounded by Picardy, Bourgogne — better known to many people as Burgundy — and Franche-Comté which follows the Swiss frontier down almost as far as Geneva.

Vineyards are a common sight throughout Champagne-Ardenne

The three provinces have a great deal in common geographically as well as historically, but at the same time each has its own special attractions. Champagne-Ardenne, for example, is a pleasing mixture of rolling plains and hills, rivers like the Seine and the Marne, lakes fringed with sand, forests and woodlands, fields of cereals and the ever-present vineyards. Below ground level is a vast network of lime-stone caves which play an important role in producing the famous sparkling wine of the area, known simply as champagne.

Lorraine-Vosges offers even more variety, ranging from the industrial north based largely on deposits of iron, coal and salt, to the Vosges mountains south-east of Nancy which provide everything from water sports, riding and walking in summer to skiing during the winter months. The province also has its fair share of rivers, the most important being the Moselle which rises just across the border in the foothills of the Vosges. It is spangled with little villages and an occasional château before it makes its way north to form the border between Germany and Luxembourg.

Although Alsace is the smallest of the three provinces it manages to combine most of their best features. Heavily-wooded mountain slopes, giving magnificent views across green valleys and distant plains, contrast sharply with an extensive patchwork of wheat fields, pastures and cultivated areas, orchards and meticulously tended vineyards. The variety of small rivers are augmented by canals including the Grand Canal d'Alsace which keeps company with the Rhine and is wider than either the Suez Canal or the Panama Canal. There are also marshy grasslands known as *rieds*, much loved by fishermen and hunters.

Each province has its own nature reserves that provide a safe haven for many different kinds of birds and animals. Wild boar roam through the woods of the Ardenne, the Forêt d'Orient is famous for its birdlife, especially waterfowl, while Alsace plays host to literally thousands of storks every year. There is no shortage of fish in the streams and rivers, nor of traditional methods of cooking them. Alsace even has its special Les Routes de la Carpe Frite (Routes of the Fried Carp) where the majority of wayside inns give pride of place on their menus to this local speciality. Trees and plants of all descriptions are also protected and the flowers, especially in the Vosges and Alsace, are magnificent. There are fields of daffodils, cherry blossom blankets the Val d'Ajol where the fruit is used later to make kirsch, and the lanes and byways are edged with banks of multicoloured wild flowers, among them such easily identified varieties as foxgloves and autumn crocus. The little villages vie with each other in a bid to win a national prize as one of the most picturesque in France, with the result that a good many of them are really beautiful.

The north-eastern corner of France is not very densely populated but there are a number of large towns and cities like Strasbourg, Reims, Metz and Mulhouse. Other important centres include Nancy, Troyes, Colmar, Charleville-Mézières and Châlons-sur-Marne, all of which have something special to offer the discerning traveller. Added to these are a host of smaller places that are well worth visiting in order to see a particular building, look round an unusual museum, watch the local craftsmen at work, sample traditional recipes or learn more about the history of the region. For instance, Thann has an impressive Gothic church, Épinal is known for its museum of colour-printing while Mirecourt is still the home of violin and guitar makers. Joan of Arc's birthplace attracts sightseers to Domrémy-la-Pucelle and Varennes-en-Argonne was where Louis XVI and Marie Antoinette were stopped on their desperate flight from Paris and escorted back to the city to face the guillotine. Students of World War I gravitate towards Verdun whereas, for anyone more interested in World War II, there are reminders of the Maginot Line, the Allied advance on Germany and even a Nazi concentration camp. Spas have grown up round several natural springs, some of them known to the Romans such as Plombières-les-Bains which is popular with people who suffer from rheumatism.

Driving from one place to another is simplicity itself. A comprehensive network of roads of various sizes, generally in good condition, stretch like a spider's web over the entire region, linking all the tiny villages on their way from one town to the next. Except for a small area south-east of Reims, which is unexpectedly short of accommodation, a great many of them have at least one *auberge* or *logi*. These are family establishments maintained to a very acceptable standard, usually devoid of frills but providing comfortable beds and traditional meals at realistic prices.

The history of all three provinces is, quite obviously, part and parcel of the overall history of France. In ancient times they were inhabited by the Celts, occupied by the Romans and overrun by a succession of invaders including the Franks and the Huns. The situation improved somewhat under Charlemagne who became king of the Franks in AD771 and founded the Holy Roman Empire, which included most of Western Europe, in AD800. However, after his death 14 years later things took a turn for the worse. Alsace was handed over to Ludwig the German in AD870 and was only reunited bit by bit with France towards the end of the seventeenth century. The rest of the region also had its problems, the most persistent of them being the Hundred Years War. It had been dragging on,

apparently interminably, when Joan of Arc was born in Lorraine in 1412. She proved to be just the inspiration her countrymen needed and, despite her untimely death in Rouen 19 years later, the English were driven back across the Channel by 1453, having lost all their French possessions apart from Calais.

As was only to be expected, the troubles that beset the country did not end there by any means. The massacre at Wassy forced Champagne into the Wars of Religion. Devastation, plague and famine were rife during the Thirty Years War after which Lorraine found itself in the hands of Stanislas Leszczynski, the dethroned king of Poland, under his title of Duc de Lorraine. Eventually the entire area was reunited just in time to play its part in the Revolution. Napoléon fought several battles in Champagne before his final defeat at Waterloo. Then, under the Treaty of Frankfurt, signed in 1871 at the end of the Franco-Prussian War, Alsace and a large part of Lorraine were handed over to Germany, which held on to them until the end of World War I. The scars of this so-called War-to-end-Wars, notably the Battles of the Marne, had barely had time to heal when Hitler's forces swept across the Maginot Line less than a quarter of a century later. On this occasion it was 5 years before north-eastern France was liberated as the Allied Armies pushed the retreating Germans back across the Rhine. These days co-operation is the name of the game. The Council of Europe, the Court of Human Rights and the European Science Foundation all have their headquarters in Strasbourg and past enmities have been forgiven if not entirely forgotten.

Despite centuries of war north-eastern France still has a great many ancient buildings, although some of the fortresses were battered into submission and then left strictly to their own devices. Ruins abound, but then so do some remarkably fine churches. Reims cathedral, where nearly all the French kings were crowned, is one of the oldest and most atmospheric in the country. Those of Strasbourg, Metz, Châlons-sur-Marne and Troyes are among many others that are especially memorable. There are medieval towns and villages, some of which have preserved their ancient walls and towers, elegant castles and châteaux, the extremely extrovert Place Stanislas in Nancy, a 3,000-year-old Pagan Wall and the impressive Grand Canal d'Alsace. There is also some attractive domestic architecture, from decorative mansions in the larger towns to half-timbered houses festooned with flowers that are a feature of the rural communities.

Musically speaking the region caters for a wide variety of tastes, including opera in Strasbourg, Metz and Nancy as well as rock, jazz and what is somewhat quaintly described as 'Music of the Future',

The vineyards of Champagne-Ardenne produce the famous sparkling wine of the area known as Champagne

although it calls its international festival The Music of Today. The Ballet Théâtre Français de Nancy prides itself on an extensive repertoire from Diaghilev to Moses Pendleton, complimenting the Ballet du Rhin in Mulhouse. However, Strasbourg has what is probably the most historic claim to fame where music is concerned. At a dinner party in 1792 Rouget de Lisle, a young officer in the engineers who was both a poet and a musician, was asked if he could write a marching song for the local troops. He worked on it all night and the following evening produced his *Battle Hymn of the Army of the Rhine*. Later it was sung by a party of Revolutionaries from southern France when they entered Paris, and again during the attack on the Tuileries. For obvious reasons they called it the *Marseillaise*, under which title it became the national anthem of France.

Museums abound in the cities, towns and villages of north-eastern France. Although they do not contain many of the country's great art treasures there are works by several acknowledged masters, some eye-catching tapestries, beautiful glass and china, religious artifacts and even gold jewellery from the time of Attila the Hun. Others are devoted to arms and armour, musical instruments, old wine presses, cars, trains and even fire engines. New villages of ancient houses have been created and supplied with furniture to show how their owners lived in times gone by.

As long ago as 1811 Brillat-Savarin described Alsace as 'the most mouth-watering region in Europe'. He was a politician and gastronome who fled to America during the Reign of Terror but returned to become a member of the French Supreme Court of Appeal. Before his death he published a book on taste which is still considered to be one of the best in existence. His opinion found favour with Antonin Caréme, the founder of *'la grande cuisine'*, who cooked for Talleyrand, Britain's Prince Regent and the Tsar of Russia among others. He insisted that one local delicacy, *brioche* with fresh *foie-gras*, was 'the most elegant of hors d'oeuvres' and few of today's gourmets have been heard to disagree with him.

All three provinces have a gratifyingly large number of excellent restaurants, a few of them in small centres which may not even have a hotel. However it is not necessary to pay top prices in order to eat well. Local specialities to look out for in addition to *brioche et fois-gras* are *baeckaoffe*, a concoction of beef, lamb and pork, marinated in white wine and cooked with onions and potatoes, pheasant with sauerkraut and grapes, and saddle of venison. Chicken in a cream and cherry sauce is delicious and so are suckling pig, Ardenne ham in various guises and tarts of all descriptions. Salmon and trout are popular options and so is *matelote de poissons* consisting of pike, tench, perch, trout and possibly eels in a wine sauce. Munster cheese is soft and delicious and may be followed by fresh fruit or perhaps a soufflé flavoured with kirsch. There are a variety of beers to choose from, Alsatian wines such as Reisling, Tokay and Gewurtztraminer go extremely well with local dishes and so, of course, does champagne. *Eaux-de-vie* (brandy-type liqueurs) come in a number of different flavours, made from the usual types of fruit like raspberries, cherries and pears or less obvious ingredients such as holly.

Souvenirs are not hard to come by, even excluding all the usual bits and pieces designed especially for tourists. Among the most useful items on offer are pottery and china articles, copper, pewter and some lovely glassware as well as linen and printed cottons. Champagne is an obvious choice, especially now that unlimited supplies for personal use can be taken from one EC country to another. The same applies to wines and liqueurs. *Foie gras* in earthenware pots is another good buy and so are Vosges honey and sugared almonds.

The whole of this region is famous for festivities of every description. Hardly a week passes without someone, somewhere, celebrating something. The main events in the principal cities tend to have an international flavour and appeal, such as the Festival of Music in Strasbourg, or historic associations like the Fête de Jeanne d'Arc in Reims. Châlons-sur-Marne holds a carnival in March, Épinal hosts the Festival International de l'Image usually about 3 months later and the Foire Européenne in Strasbourg takes place in September. The celebrations in the smaller centres are frequently more traditional. A variety of flowers, among them daffodils, lily-of-the-valley and roses all have their special days. There are processions and pilgrimages, wine fairs and beer festivals, equestrian events and fêtes devoted to folklore at which many people appear in traditional costumes.

Visitors with little or no interest in art, architecture, museums or history will still find plenty to do in this part of France. There are cruises up the Rhine and boating on some of the bigger lakes, as well as canoeing and fishing, windsurfing and swimming. It is possible to play golf or tennis, set off on horseback to explore a variety of bridle paths or go for a ride on a little local train. People who enjoy a gentle stroll can take their pick of dozens of different footpaths, leaving more energetic sightseers to clamber up mountainsides to inspect antiquated ruins or admire the view from the top. For long distance walkers there are the *Grandes Randonnées* options, part of the formidable network that covers the whole country and provides ample opportunities for hikers who prefer to travel than to arrive. Finally in winter, there is skiing up in the Vosges mountains, with clearly marked cross-country trails, ski lifts and hoists and purpose-built hotels.

1

CHAMPAGNE-ARDENNE

F our separate *départements* — Ardennes, Marne, Aube and Haute-Marne — together make up the province of Champagne-Ardenne, which looks a little like a huge bedsock with its toe pointing in the direction of Switzerland. The most northerly of them is Ardennes, which means 'Deep Forest' in Celtic, and still does its best to live up to this description. It shares a common border with Belgium to the north, is sandwiched in between the provinces of Picardy and Lorraine-Vosges and adjoins Marne in the south. Marne, in its turn, also has Picardy and Lorraine-Vosges as neighbours and is bordered to the south by Aube and Haute-Marne. Both of these share a common border with Burgundy although Haute-Marne carries on below the Vosges to join up with Franche-Comté.

Champagne-Ardenne, the most westerly province in the region, is essentially a happy blending of historic towns and peaceful landscapes. There are meadows threaded through with canals and rivers, wooded hillsides, shimmering lakes, fields of cereals and regimented vineyards. Below the surface a vast complex of natural limestone caves is used in the preparation of the famous vin de Champagne (wine of Champagne). Foremost among the towns are Reims, known as the Coronation City, Troyes with its immaculately restored half-timbered houses, fortified centres like Sedan and Langres, the thermal resort of Bourbonne-les-Bains and modern playgrounds such as Griffaumont on the Lac du Der-Chantecoq. Added to these are a host of picturesque villages, each with something special to recommend it, nature parks, prehistoric sites, strange distorted trees and petrified waterfalls.

The province, like so many others in France, believes in celebrating as enthusiastically and as frequently as possible. Almost anything provides an excuse, such as cheese or lily-of-the-valley in Chaource,

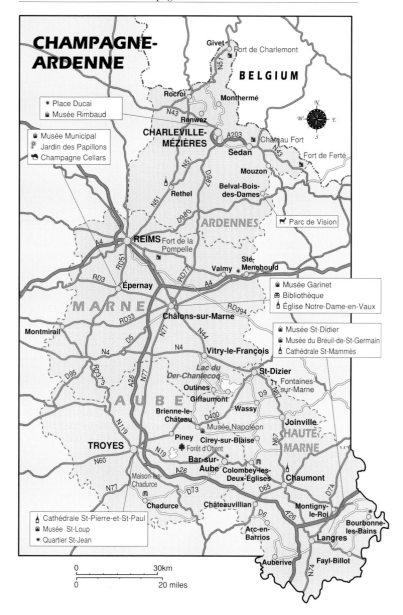

CHAMPAGNE-ARDENNE

Givet
Fort de Charlemont
N51
BELGIUM

Rocroi
Monthermé

* Place Ducai
☖ Musée Rimbaud

N43
Renwez
A203
Château Fort
N43

☖ Musée Municipal
🦋 Jardin des Papillons
🍾 Champagne Cellars

CHARLEVILLE-MÉZIÈRES
Sedan
Fort de Ferté

N51
Mouzon

Rethel
Belval-Bois-des-Dames

D987
ARDENNES

D980
🦌 Parc de Vision

REIMS Fort de la Pompelle

A4
Ste-Menehould
Valmy *

RD51
RD77

RD3
Épernay

☖ Musée Garinet
⊞ Bibliothèque
⛪ Église Notre-Dame-en-Vaux

M A R N E
RD33
RD394
Châlons-sur-Marne

☖ Musée St-Didier
☖ Musée du Breuil-de-St-Germain
⛪ Cathédrale St-Mammès

Montmirail
D5
N77
N44
N4
Vitry-le-François

D95
RD373
A26
N77
N119
Lac du Der-Chantecoq
St-Dizier
Fontaines-sur-Marne

Outines
D9
Giffaumont
Wassy
D400
Joinville

A U B E
Brienne-le-Château
Musée Napoléon
N67
HAUTE-MARNE

Piney
Cirey-sur-Blaise
N19
Forêt d'Orient

TROYES
N60
Bar-sur-Aube
Colombey-les-Deux-Églises
Chaumont

N19
Maison-les-Chadurce
N26

N77
D73
D65
D74

Chadurce
Châteauvillian
Montigny-le-Roi

D6
A26
⛪ Cathédrale St-Pierre-et-St-Paul
☖ Musée St-Loup
* Quartier St-Jean

Arc-en-Barrios
Bourbonne-les-Bains
Langres
Auberive
Fayl-Billot
N74

0   30km

0   20 miles

roses or onions in Givet, ham in Troyes and, of course, champagne almost anywhere where the grapes are harvested. Then there are pilgrimages, fêtes and various spectacles involving *son et lumière*. All this is hardly surprising because Champagne was renowned for its fairs as long ago as the Middle Ages.

In those days hundreds of foreign merchants were attracted to the most important of these trade events which usually lasted for weeks on end and were held at least six times a year. Buyers flooded in from all over Europe to stock up with linen and furs from Germany, wool from England, leather from Spain and North Africa and Mediterranean spices of all descriptions.

Because it was a poor agricultural area, and had come to rely almost entirely on banking for its prosperity, Champagne went into a decline when trade started to fall away, due in no small measure to the outbreak of the Hundred Years War. Nor did its position improve when Isabel of Bavaria, the wife of Charles VI, signed the Treaty of Troyes in the spring of 1420, making Henry V of England heir to the throne of France. The Dauphin naturally resented this and, encouraged by Joan of Arc, was crowned Charles VII in the cathedral at Reims in 1429. Once the English had been driven out strenuous efforts were made to improve the economy, but one war led to another. The region was already in the firing line between France and Austria when the Catholic followers of François de Guise massacred the Protestant inhabitants of the small town of Wassy, thereby sparking off the Wars of Religion which went on for more than 30 years.

Towards the end of the seventeenth century a certain Benedictine monk, by name Dom Pérignon, is said to have perfected the art of making a delicious sparkling wine and this, coupled with metallurgy and the manufacture of textiles, brought new prosperity to Champagne. Even the fact that a certain Napoléon Bonaparte was studying at the military college in Brienne-le-Château seemed to have little significence. However, once the Revolution was under way, and Louis XVI and his family had been arrested at Varennes-en-Argonne and escorted back to Paris and the guillotine, the province once again found itself in the thick of things. The French and Allied forces swarmed about all over the area until Napoléon abdicated at Fontainebleau in April 1814, but less than 60 years later fighting broke out again during the Franco-Prussian War. Nor was the Prussian victory in 1871 the end of the story for Champagne. With the outbreak of World War I in 1914 hostilities between France and Germany were resumed, but this time France had powerful allies and peace returned with the defeat of Germany at the second Battle of the Marne in 1918. However it was only a brief interlude. Less than a quarter of a century later Hitler's armies invaded Holland, Belgium and Luxembourg, outflanked the Maginot Line and moved on into France until they were eventually driven out by the Allies in the closing stages of the War in Europe which ended in 1945.

Since its liberation Champagne-Ardenne has been able to concentrate on far more peaceful matters. It has built up its industries, created new lakes and leisure resorts, set aside areas for nature parks and bird sanctuaries, restored its architectural treasures and, of course, produced vast quantities of its famous vin de Champagne. For some reason the province has not produced very much in the way of music, either traditional or modern, although this is being counteracted to a certain extent by the Yehudi Menuhin Foundation which organises a series of promenade concerts in Reims.

Champagne-Ardenne is no match for Alsace when it comes to exotic recipes, concocted by famous chefs in days gone by, but, nevertheless, it can offer a selection of regional dishes that are certainly worth trying. Among them are ham and game from the Ardennes, *trout à la crème* in the Haute-Marne, meat pies and pâtés, chitterlings sausages and a distinctive stew called *potée champenoise*. *Chaource*, *Langres*, *Caprice des Dieux* and *Cendre de Champagne* are all popular cheeses, whereas anyone who prefers sweets has a choice of fruit tarts, *croquignols*, marzipan and the rose-pink biscuits that are associated with Reims. When it comes to wines and spirits champagne obviously tops the list but it is not by any means the only option. Ratafia, Marc de Champagne and Fine de Marne are all derived from it. Then there are other wines, fruit brandies such as *prunelle* which is made from plums, cider and an occasional unlikely liqueur such as *noisette*, one of the ingredients being nuts.

Probably the best place to try any of the local dishes is at a *logi* or an *auberge*, particularly one that makes a feature of regional specialities. These small country hotels, where the husband is usually the chef and the wife looks after the accommodation, are very plentiful and can be relied upon to reach an acceptable standard without necessarily running to any additional frills and flounces. Further down the list are what are known as *hebergements collectifs* which are somewhat in the nature of boarding houses, but when they include the word *jeunesse*, are reserved for young people. Meanwhile anyone in search of up-market accommodation and outstanding restaurants will discover them in cities like Reims and Troyes, augmented by comfortable establishments in several of the larger towns, such as Châlons-sur-Marne, St-Dizier and Charleville-Mézières. People travelling with their own tents or caravans will find sites ranging from one-star to four-star with plenty of options in between.

Any number of roads converge on Champagne-Ardenne from every direction, the most important being the A4 *autoroute*, connecting Reims with Paris, 146km (91 miles) away, and with Strasbourg, 347km (215 miles) to the east. For visitors arriving at the Channel ports the A26 *autoroute* also heads for Reims from Calais, an easy journey covering a distance of 300km (186 miles) which makes it a good idea to start a visit to north-eastern France in Marne.

MARNE

The *département* of Marne is, both literally and figuratively, at the heart of Champagne-Ardenne, with Reims and Épernay competing for the title of 'champagne capital'. The area all round is smothered in vineyards, arranged in seemingly endless parallel lines which create a vivid green blanket over the countryside in spring and summer but change to spectacular autumn colours before the onset of winter. However there is more to Marne than just vineyards. Cereals are grown on the large chalky plain in the middle, the vast Lac du Der-Chantecoq, which it shares with Haute-Marne, is the biggest artificial lake in Europe and the woods, etched with paths and byways for walkers, horse riders and cyclists, are full of birds and animals.

✳ Most visitors would want to spend at least a day or two in **Reims**, exploring the historic old city and visiting some of the famous champagne cellars that are open to the public. There is certainly no shortage of hotels, the most outstanding being the Boyer les Crayères on the Boulevard Henry Vasnier, ☎ 26 82 80 80. It overlooks a large park, is in close touch with quite a few cellars and has an exceptionally fine restaurant. Among others which are both comfortable and convenient are the Hotel Altea in the Boulevard Paul Doumer, ☎ 26 88 53 54 and the Hotel de la Paix on the Rue Buirette, ☎ 26 40 04 08. In addition there are a host of smaller, less expensive establishments, some without dining rooms, but this is not a serious drawback because the city is packed with a variety of different places to eat. They range from up-market restaurants to modest little examples like Le Forum in the Place du Forum where Roman citizens used to gather some 2,000 years ago.

In its early days Reims, or *Durocortorum* as it was then, belonged to the Rèmes, a Gaulish tribe of warriors and traders who looked on it as their capital. Once the Romans arrived the Rèmes threw in their lot with Caesar and in return their city was promoted to the status of capital of the imperial province of *Belgica*, and building was resumed

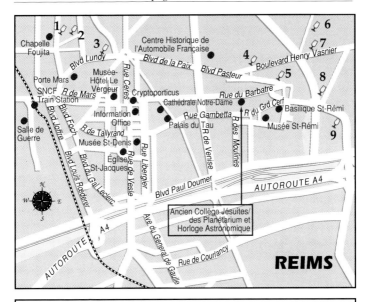

Key To The Champagne Cellars

1 Mumm

2 Heidsieck and Monopole

3 Lanson

4 Piper Heidsieck

5 Taittinger

6 Ruinart

7 Pommery

8 Charles Heidsieck

9 Veuve Clicquot Ponsardin

in earnest. Very little remains from this period apart from the huge triumphal Arch of Mars, said to have been the largest anywhere in the Roman Empire, and the Gallo-Roman Cryptoporticus in the forum, dating back to AD200.

In due course the worship of gods like Jupiter was replaced by Christianity. The first cathedral was built in AD401 by St-Nicasius, who was murdered by Vandals on the steps shortly afterwards, and less than a hundred years later it was chosen by St-Remi for the baptism of Clovis, the Frankish chief who is often described as the first king of France. The original church was replaced by a more imposing one after about four centuries but it was destroyed by fire in 1210. Work started immediately on the present Cathédrale Notre-Dame which, in memory of Clovis, became the accepted venue for a long and impressive series of coronations. Among the many French kings to be crowned there was Charles VII, aided and abetted by Joan of Arc after she had fought her way through the English lines. The tradition was obviously suspended during the Revolution but, after it had been revived briefly following the defeat of Napoléon in 1815, it eventually ended with the coronation of Charles X nine years later.

The present **cathedral** has rightly been described as a Gothic masterpiece, solidly constructed, festooned with decorative stone-work and adorned with statues. The façade is extremely impressive. Its three ornate doorways, opening into the triple naves, are watched over by a company of tall figures with the Virgin Mary in the centre and the famous Smiling Angel of Reims tucked away in the far left-hand corner. The interior is remarkable for its lack of clutter which adds to the impression of grandeur and spaciousness. Although there are a few statues and some fine sixteenth-century tapestries, its most compelling feature is the stained glass, some of which, like the two rose windows in the west front, dates from the thirteenth century. However, a great deal was destroyed in two World Wars and the sapphire gleam at the far end owes its existence to Marc Chagall. This famous artist, whose fanciful paintings caught the attention of a Paris art dealer in 1922, only became interested in stained glass in his early sixties. He was well into his eighties when he created the trio of windows for Reims cathedral, refusing to accept any payment but setting his personal seal on them by using a tremendous amount of the vivid colour known as Chagall blue.

Most of the cathedral treasures, including a number of statues that were replaced by copies in order to preserve them, are housed in the **Palais du Tau** next door. This was originally the bishops' palace, although one of its more recent owners was apparently Charles X. Many of the vestments and other items used at his coronation, and those of his predecessors, are on display in a succession of rooms including the former banqueting hall, or Salle du Tau, leading to the treasury. In addition there are some fine embroideries, sculptures of various sizes, and a good many interesting tapestries, as well as photographs showing the damage caused by war. The cathedral treasure includes a fragment of the True Cross that belonged to Charlemagne, assorted reliquaries and goblets, the collar of the Order of St-Esprit worn by Louis-Philippe, and chandeliers in the chapel that were made especially for the marriage of Napoléon and Marie-Louise.

Just a block away from the cathedral, on the Rue Libergier, the **Musée St-Denis** is an art gallery housed in an eighteenth-century building that once belonged to the church. Although many of the contents could hardly be described as famous masterpieces they do cover the whole period from the Renaissance to the present day and include works by a long list of celebrated artists. Corot, Boucher, Rousseau and Millet are all represented, as are Impressionists such as Pissaro, Monet and Renoir and contemporary painters like Matisse and Picasso.

The nearby **Église St-Jacques** is mildly viewable while, further afield, the Hôtel de la Salle, on the Place du Forum, is a decorative sixteenth-century mansion where St-Jean-Baptiste de la Salle, the founder of the Frères des Écoles, was born in 1651. However it is a relative newcomer when compared with the adjacent **Crypto-porticus**, now consisting of only one of three large galleries built in the heart of the old Gallo-Roman city nearly 2,000 years ago. Another of its closest neighbours is the **Musée-Hôtel Le Vergeur**, a thirteenth-century town house that was refurbished and up-dated quite regularly before being largely demolished in 1914. It was reconstructed out of all the bits and pieces left lying about and was taken over in 1935 by the Friends of Old Reims who filled it with antique furniture, a set of excellent engravings by Dürer and documents relating to the history of the city.

Beyond the Place du Forum, at the far end of the Rue de Mars, the massive Arc de Triomphe, known as the **Porte Mars**, was built in honour of the Emperor Augustus at some time towards the end of the third century AD. It consists of three enormous arches, embellished with figures of Roman gods like Jupiter and legendary characters such as Romulus and Remus, none of which have successfully escaped the ravages of time. In the Middle Ages the Mars Gate formed part of the ramparts and later it was given an iron grille to celebrate the coronation of Louis XIV.

In the opposite direction from the Porte Mars, and about the same distance from the cathedral, is the **Ancien Collège des Jésuites**, between the Rue Gambetta and the Rue du Barbatre. It dates from the early seventeenth century when Henri IV gave the Jesuits permission to found a college in Reims. It is a lovely old building with some 300-year-old vines in the courtyard overlooked by the refectory and the old kitchens. A grand staircase leads up to the library where French Baroque art was allowed to run rampant. The original Salle d'Astronomie has been fitted out as a planetarium and contains an astronomical clock.

A touch further on, just off the Rue du Grand-Cerf, facing on to the Rue Simon, are the **Basilique St-Rémi** and its attendant museum. The basilica, the largest Romanesque church in northern France, started life in AD533 as a modest chapel dedicated to St-Christopher.

The Porte Mars (Mars Gate) at Reims built by the Romans in AD200

Reims cathedral is festooned with decorative stone-work and adorned with statues

In due course the Benedictine Abbaye de St-Rémi was founded and the chapel was replaced by a more imposing building to house the tomb of the saint. However, even this seemed inadequate at the end of the twelfth century so the Abbot Pierre de Celles had the whole of the west front and the chancel reconstructed on early Gothic lines. His ideas prove so successful that the building has been allowed to remain virtually unchanged, apart from a minor alteration here and there. Unfortunately some repairs were necessary to counteract the damage caused when it was used as a warehouse during the Revolution.

The **Musée St-Rémi**, just next door, is equally splendid but not nearly so old. It was built in the seventeenth and eighteenth centuries to replace the original abbey and is now the city's museum of history and archaeology. The exhibits hark back to the old days in *Durocortorum* and include Roman relics like a sarcophagus, which was apparently the tomb of Jovin, and some very worthwhile mosaics. A splendid staircase leads up to a gallery hung with tapestries recalling the life and miracles of St-Rémi which were ordered especially for the basilica by the Archbishop Robert de Lenoncourt in 1523. Also on display are some enamels from Limousin, the reconstructed façade of a Musicians House from the thirteenth century and an enviable collection of arms covering a period of about 400 years.

Foremost among the more modern buildings in Reims is the **Hôtel de Ville** which had to be rebuilt in 1917 following a disastrous fire. However, most of the seventeenth-century façade has been restored and still has an equestrian statue of Louis XIII as its centrepiece. Not too far away, beyond the Porte Mars, and just off the Avenue de Laon in the Rue du Franklin-Roosevelt behind the station, is the historic **Salle de Guerre**. This was the map room of General Eisenhower's headquarters in the closing stages of the War in Europe where the German surrender was signed on 7 May 1945. Although all the documents have naturally been removed, the long table and some very businesslike chairs are still in place and the walls are covered with the original maps showing the different battle areas.

Another, even more recent arrival, is the **Chapelle Foujita** on the Rue du Champ de Mars. It was designed and decorated by the Japanese painter Léonard Foujita after he had been converted to Christianity and baptised in Reims cathedral. The chapel was built by his godfather, René Lalou, to mark the event and was dedicated to Our Lady of Peace shortly before the painter died in 1968. Another place of special interest is the **Centre Historique de l'Automobile Française** on the Avenue Georges Clemenceau. It traces the history of the French automobile industry from 1769 to the present day and, apart from all the models on show, it has gathered together a collection of more than 2,000 toy cars of all descriptions.

❄   Last, but by no means least, there are the champagne cellars, quite a few of which are grouped around the Place du Général Gouraud beyond the Basilique St-Remi. They belong to such famous houses as Pommery, which literally overlooks the square, Taittinger on the nearby Place St-Nicaise, Piper Heidsieck on the Boulevard Henry Vasnier, Veuve Clicquot-Ponsardin in the Place des Droits de l'Homme and the oldest of them all, Ruinart, in the Rue des Crayères. Other houses like Mumm and Lanson have caves closer to the Porte Mars while the remainder are a trifle further away.

Most of these cellars are open to visitors, some at specified times and others by appointment only. However, as even the designated times may vary for a number of different reasons, it is as well to telephone in advance (see Additional Information section at the end of this chapter). Each house has its own history, individual procedures and special blends, as well as different methods of showing visitors round its labyrinth of natural caves underneath the city. For example, one house may start with a film show while another makes things easier by using a small train for its conducted tours. At the same time they all have experienced guides who can explain the whole process in several different languages, as and when required.

Basically the procedure is the same in every case. Apart from the gigantic vats, there are literally millions of bottles of wine stored in racks for three or more years, during which time the temperature and the humidity are kept constant to allow the contents to ferment and develop their sparkle. Each bottle is rotated very slightly every day by a 'mover' who takes about 4 years to learn the job and is quite highly paid. Eventually the bottles are turned upside down to allow the sediment to collect in the neck where it is frozen on to the cork and so can be removed quite easily. None of the tours could be described as exhausting but nevertheless most visitors appreciate a little light refreshment afterwards.

Apart from walking through the Place Royale, dedicated to Louis XV whose statue stands in the middle, and inspecting the elegant shopping streets all round, it is necessary to have a car, or join an organised outing, to visit other attractions in the vicinity. One of these is the **Fort de la Pompelle**, about 10km (6 miles) away to the south-east along the road to Châlons-sur-Marne. Built in 1880 to protect the city, the fortress withstood every German attack during the battles of the Marne and now has a comprehensive museum full of reminders of the fighting that took place in the area during World War I.

Stretching away into the distance is the **Parc Naturel Régional de** **la Montagne de Reims** which was created in 1976 to preserve the essential character of the countryside lying between Reims, Châlons-sur-Marne and Épernay. It includes a number of little hamlets, farmlands, pastures, vineyards and forests and is a delightful place to explore on foot. Among its somewhat unexpected landmarks are the old windmill at Verzenay and the Mount Sinaï observatory which has a fine view of Reims and its plateau. However the park's most extraordinary feature is the nearby Faux de Verzy, a collection of elderly beech trees whose trunks and branches have grown into weird, tortured shapes that would surely have delighted Salvador Dali.

At the opposite end of the Parc Régional is **Épernay** which, for motorists who are in a hurry, is only 27km (17 miles) from Reims along the well signposted Route du Champagne. This meanders its way through a sea of vineyards, calling at such appropriately named villages as Dizy and Bouzy. Épernay itself is a pretty little place almost totally preoccupied with the production of champagne, although it does have a number of other things to recommend it. For example, there are hotels for people who would like to use it as a base for touring the surrounding area. The best of these is probably the Hôtel des Berceaux, in a quiet side street of the same name, ☎ 26 55 28 84, with simple rooms and a choice between light meals in the wine bar and more expensive ones in the dining room. However, there are also two comfortable establishments within a radius of 6km (4 miles) — the Royal Champagne at Champillon to the north, ☎ 26 51 11 51, and the Hostellerie de la Briqueterie on the Route de Sézanne at Vinay further south, ☎ 26 54 11 22.

Épernay is the home of Moët et Chandon, founded in 1743 by Claude Moët whose son, Jean Rémy, was friendly with Napoléon. This accounts for the fact that they built a special house for the use of the Emperor and his attendants whenever he paid them one of his periodical visits. There is also a statue of the monk Dom Pérignon, the so-called Father of Champagne, who is still regarded as a proprietor. He is said to have perfected the art of making the local sparkling wine at the Benedictine Abbey of **Hautvillers**, 6km (4 miles) to the north. It is a charming little village with the remains of the abbey, founded in AD660 by St-Nivard, and some most intriguing wrought iron signs. Mercier, which came into being somewhat later than Moët et Chandon, also has its roots in Épernay and weighs in with a museum full of antiquated wine presses and a small electric train that takes visitors round the underground cellars.

The Musée Municipal, housed in the eye-catching Château Perrier on the Avenue de Champagne, devotes most of its attention to the history of grapes and wine. However, it does manage to find space for a few tombs and some ancient pottery and glass as well as a selection of weapons and an assortment of antiquated jewellery. A good deal further along the Avenue de Champagne is the Jardin des Papillons where a variety of really beautiful butterflies have free run of a large airy enclosure filled with exotic plants.

Châlons-sur-Marne, 44km (27 miles) from Reims along the N44, is decidedly atmospheric with its perfectly restored half-timbered houses, ancient bridges and picturesque canals. In its youth the town had a difference of opinion with Attila the Hun whose forces were halted on the adjoining plains near a spot called the Camp d'Attila. It is about 15km (9 miles) to the north-east and is believed to be where the barbaric hordes set up their camp prior to the battle. With the passage of time Châlons grew and prospered until, in 1589, Henri III described it as the most important town in Champagne. As a result it became the administrative capital and therefore attracted a good deal of unwelcome attention whenever fighting broke out in the area.

As is the case with so many ancient cities, the outstanding attractions are, for the most part, concentrated in a relatively small area within easy reach of the Cathédrale St-Étienne. This is not the most

The Basilique Notre-Dame de L'Épine

Basketware in L'Épine, one of the cottage industries of Champagne-Ardenne

impressive building of its kind in the region despite the fact that it has a number of fine stained glass windows. Nor could the items in its treasury be described as particularly noteworthy. There is, in fact, more to hold the visitor's attention in the Bibliothèque on the Place Maréchal Foch at the far end of the Rue de la Marne. This is said to be one of the finest public libraries in France and contains, among other things, illustrated manuscripts of the Confessions of St Augustus, some very early printed books illustrated with wood engravings and a prayer book inscribed by Marie Antoinette on the morning of her execution. The library adjoins the Hôtel de Ville and looks across at the delightful little Église St-Alpin which dates back to the twelfth century. The Musée Municipal is located immediately behind the library and tends to be a trifle disappointing, although its exhibits range from archaeology to sacred art and paintings. On the other hand the Musée Garinet, a short stroll away in the Rue Pasteur, is known for its models of French cathedrals, exhibits connected with the Battle of Valmy, the first victory of the Revolution, and the interest it shows in Schiller and Goethe.

The Église Notre-Dame-en-Vaux, in the Rue de Vaux, is an attractive mixture of the Romanesque and Gothic styles although its finer points were either damaged or destroyed during the Revolution. It is well proportioned but somewhat austere inside with a variety of stained glass windows that do their utmost to redress the balance. The cloister is amazingly extrovert by comparison with a great many sculptured pillars whose figures represent saints and prophets as well as kings and martyrs. There are several other small churches dotted about in addition to a handful of medieval bridges and some attractive gardens. One of these, Le Jard, has changed considerably since St Bernard preached there in 1147, the Avenue Général Leclerc having been driven through the middle. Nevertheless, it is worth visiting for the view across to the cathedral, the floral clock and Le Jardin Anglais, laid out along the river bank in 1817.

Châlons-sur-Marne's other attractions are rather less obvious, such as the enormous paved map in the Forum de l'Europe, the École Nationale Superieure des Arts du Cirque where acrobats are put through their paces and the excitement generated by the annual Carnival in March. Among the various places to stay is the Hotel Angleterre on the Place Monseigneur Tissier, close to the Église Notre-Dame-en-Vaux, which is both traditional and comfortable and has an excellent restaurant, ☎ 26 68 21 51. An equally good choice would be the old coaching inn, Aux Armes de Champagne, ☎ 26 68 10 43, in **L'Épine**, a trifle over 8km (5 miles) away to the east on the N3. Although the hotel is on the main road it is quiet with some rooms on the ground floor, a small garden, mini-golf and parking for the car. What is more, it has an uninterrupted view of the magnificent basilica of Notre-Dame that was an important place of pilgrimage in the Middle Ages. It is an exceptionally beautiful sight with its towering spires, delicate stone tracery and fascinatingly realistic gargoyles, particularly when the whole building is floodlit on summer nights.

Anyone travelling eastwards from Châlons-sur-Marne towards Verdun will find two places of historic interest along the way. The little village of **Valmy** almost marks the spot near the Forêt d'Argonne where the French Revolutionary forces won their first battle against the Prussians in 1792. The famous windmill overlooking the site was restored in 1947 and has an orientation table indicating the position of the opposing armies before the event, which is one of the most important dates in the Republican calendar. Ironically, Valmy is only a few kilometres from **Ste-Menehould** where, less than 18 months earlier, Louis XVI and his family were recognised by the son of the posthouse keeper when they stopped to change horses on their flight from Paris. He alerted the members of the National Guard who were searching for the fugitives and so gained for himself an unexpected place in history. The posthouse where it all happened has been replaced by the police station but the thirteenth-century Église Notre-Dame that was once attached to the château is still there, as are a number of elderly houses and the pink brick and stone Hôtel de Ville. The town is especially popular with holidaymakers who want to explore the Argonne Massif on foot and also with gourmets who enjoy pigs trotters cooked in the traditional manner.

If the mixture of churches, châteaux and champagne becomes a trifle indigestible the best thing to do is head south along the N4 to spend a day in the open air. At **Vitry-le-François**, which was almost completely destroyed during World War II, there is a turning off along the D13 to the **Lac du Der-Chantecoq**, a vast expanse of water that is rapidly being developed into a first class leisure centre. It is an ideal place to relax, sail, swim, windsurf or waterski. Less energetic visitors can take a boat trip round the lake from **Giffaumont**, a small waterside hamlet that has every intention of growing into a thriving holiday playground. Its main drawback at the moment is the almost complete lack of hotels, although there is quite an acceptable camp site which is open from early May until mid-September. Anyone in search of a room for the night could try one of the few modest establishments in Vitry-le-François. Quite apart from water sports, bird watching and walking, there are plenty of other things to do in the vicinity. For example, it is possible to study the art of beekeeping

The famous windmill at Valmy on the site of a battle between the French and the Prussians in 1792

A typical house in the museum-village of Ste-Marie-du-Lac-Nuisement

at La Grange aux Abeilles, inspect the half-timbered church at **Châtillon-sur-Broué**, or drive a little further down the D55 to **Outines**, which has an even larger one built on roughly the same lines with the addition of a stained glass rose window. On the opposite side of the lake, **Ste-Marie-du-Lac-Nuisement** is, in fact, a full sized museum-village, filled with typical buildings that have been reconstructed on the site to preserve the architecture, crafts and traditions of the area.

Having seen all there is to see motorists can either return to Vitry-le-François en route for Châlons-sur-Marne or carry on round the lake to join the D384 to St-Dizier, across the invisible border in Haute-Marne.

ARDENNES

Ardennes is by no means the most appealing *département* in north-eastern France from the average sightseer's point of view. It is really better suited to cyclists, people exploring on horseback or in boats, or even holidaymakers travelling on foot, than it is to motorists in search of splendid architecture and interesting museums. Its forests, full of birds and animals, may well give hikers a brief glimpse of a wild boar busy escorting its young family through the undergrowth. The lakes with their sandy beaches are frequented mainly by local fishermen, windsurfers and people out for a picnic or simply messing about in boats. For the historically minded there are one or two ancient fortresses and just a hint of the Maginot Line, but comprehensive museums are few and far between while elegant châteaux are conspicuous by their absence. However, one point in its favour is that the area is easily accessible from almost any direction because there are major roads connecting it with Aisne to the east, Marne in the south, Meuse across the invisible border with Lorraine and, finally, Belgium to the north.

The main town is **Charleville-Mézières** which started out as two separate entities, with the River Meuse meandering about in the vicinity, before they decided to join forces in 1966. Mézières is the older of the two, having been a Gallo-Roman settlement and an important frontier post before Charles de Gonzague made up his mind to replace the nearby village of Arches with a new town which he proposed to call Charleville. As in previous years the local interests tended to be more military and administrative than artistic, so the minimum amount of time was wasted on decorating the buildings or brightening up little squares with flowers and fountains. Today the atmosphere is still essentially businesslike with no luxury hotels and most of the smaller variety conveniently grouped round the railway station. However, visitors can opt for the Mercure, 5km (3 miles) away on the road to Sedan, which is comfortable, has a restaurant, a garden and a swimming pool and makes provision for disabled guests, ☎ 24 37 55 29.

There is not a great deal to see in Charleville apart from the much publicised Place Ducal, which is a replica of the Place des Vosges in Paris. It has its obligatory arcades lined with restaurants and little shops, a nineteenth-century Hôtel de Ville, built on the site of the old ducal palace, and a statue of Charles de Gonzague in the middle to remind everyone that he founded the town in 1606. Two blocks away, down the Rue du Moulin, is a mansion complete with Ionic columns, overlooking the river and known for some obscure reason as Le Vieux Moulin. It contains two quite modest museums, the Musée Ardenne and the Musée Rimbaud. The latter is filled with items connected with the poet Arthur Rimbaud who has been officially described on at least one occasion as the city's enfant terrible. He lived for a while quite close to Le Vieux Moulin before setting off for foreign parts, mainly the Middle East and Indonesia, but died in hospital in Marseille in 1891 at the age of 37 and was brought back to Charleville for burial.

Mézières, across its own bend of the river, clings on to the rather sparse remains of its sixteenth-century ramparts almost, but not quite, enclosing the Basilique Notre-Dame d'Esperance. Apart from the fact that Charles IX and Elizabeth of Austria were married here, the church would have very little to boast about if it were not for its sixty-six modern stained glass windows. On the other hand Charleville-Mézières has every right to be proud of its unique World Festival of Puppet Theatre, held every 3 years, the next occasion being at the end of September 1994. The whole idea started half a century ago with a group of amateurs who called themselves The Little Ragdoll Comedians. They sent out invitations to their first show and since that time the festival has gone from strength to strength. On the last occasion it continued for 10 days, included puppeteers from thirty-seven different countries and attracted more than 80,000 spectators from all over the world.

There are one or two places to visit in the surrounding countryside such as **Warcq**, on the D16, with its old fortified church, and **Renwez** which revolves round its Musée de la Forêt and is committed to keeping alive traditional occupations like making grindstones and charcoal burning, holding lumberjack competitions and indulging in the ancient art of storytelling. It is also within easy reach of the ruined Château de Montcornet-en-Ardenne and the Lac des Vieilles

Forges, an expanding holiday area that can provide some fishing and a variety of water sports.

About 12km (7 miles) to the north-west, via the D31 and the D22, **Rocroi** is both larger and more historic. It was the scene of an important battle in 1643 which ended in a defeat for the Spanish led by Dom Francisco Mellos and a lot of praise for the young Duc d'Enghien, who was better known later as the Grand Condé. The whole story of the encounter is retold in an imaginative little mu- seum, appropriately housed in the ancient guardroom. The extremely well preserved star-shaped fortifications date in part from 1555 but they were adapted more than a century later by Vauban as part of the impressive line of defences he either rebuilt or improved upon during the reign of Louis XIV. One of the best ways to appreciate this interesting little town is to take a walk along the ramparts, especially during the Spectacle Historique held on the third Sunday in September. It may be difficult at this time to find a room in either of the modest hotels, or even somewhere to pitch a tent or park a caravan on any of the three local camp sites.

North of Rocroi, Ardennes makes a brief fingerlike sortie into Belgium as far as **Givet**, an ancient frontier town that is almost overwhelmed by the massive fortress of Charlemont, built in 1555 by Charles V. It is entirely functional, without anything in the way of decorations, and fulfilled its purpose so efficiently that Napoléon's forces were able to hold on to it in the face of repeated attacks, thereby retaining Givet for France. Other places that can be visited are the Tour Victoire, left over from a medieval château that belonged to the Comtes de la Marck, the Forge Toussaint on the Quai de Meuse, which was in operation until about 1950, and the Grottes de Nichet, 4km (2 miles) to the east, consisting of a number of fairly predictable caves on three different levels.

Motorists with some extra time in hand can stop off by arrange- ment at the nuclear power station at **Chooz** or inspect the nearby ruined Château de Hierges, fractionally off the N51. Slightly further to the south there is just a trace of an old Roman camp at **Vireux-Molhain**, after which the route keeps company with the river to **Haybes-sur-Meuse**. This is quite an attractive little place with minor roads leading off to the vantage points of La Platale and the Roc de Fépin.

Revin, caught in a series of tortuous S-bends created by the river further upstream, has nothing very much to recommend it apart from the nearby Mont Malgré Tout which captured the imagination of George Sand in 1896 and has a rather splendid view. It also has an early forge that is open to visitors, celebrates with a Bread Festival in

A bridge spanning the River Meuse, links the two towns of Charleville-Mézières

The main entrance to the fortress at Sedan

the late spring and can offer visitors a choice between two small hotels and a camp site. One of the most picturesque stretches of the River Meuse lies between Revin and Charleville-Mézières, wandering about in a disconcerted fashion like some giant blue ribbon trying to find a way through the wooded hills. On the way it passes some strange rock formations, drifts round the elderly village of **Monthermé**, with its antiquated Église St-Leger, which is a favourite meeting place for climbers, and then takes a more direct route past the industrial centre of Nouzonville for the final part of the journey.

The A203 is a tiny strip of *autoroute* linking Charleville-Mézières with **Sedan**, 24km (15 miles) to the east. The town has been a major stronghold since the eleventh century and has fought its way in and out of trouble for the past 900 years. Every time it was attacked, which was at depressingly frequent intervals, the fortress was strengthened by adding an extra section here and there or increasing its height with another storey, until today it claims to be the most extended example of this type of military architecture anywhere in Europe. Legend has it that the town was named after Sedanus, the son of Bazon who was an early Gaulish king, but dropped the last two letters at the end of the tenth century. It belonged for a while to the Abbaye de Mouzon, passed into the hands of the Comtes de la Marck and later was handed over to France. The town became a refuge for Protestants who were hounded during the Wars of Religion, suffered at the hands of the Prussians in 1870 and was occupied in two World Wars.

Sedan's most famous inhabitant was the Vicomte de Turenne whose grandfather was William the Silent. He joined the French army in 1630, at the age of 19, supported the rebels during the early stages of the civil wars of the Fronde but then joined Mazarin and led the royal forces to victory. During the reign of Louis XIV he proved himself to be an outstanding army commander until he was killed in action at the Battle of Sasbach in 1675. Five years later Napoléon ordered his remains to be removed from St-Denis and reburied in Les Invalides in Paris. A guided tour of the fortress lasts for more than an hour and takes in the private apartments that belonged to the La Tour d'Auvergne family, including a room thought to have been occupied by Turenne's mother when he was born. Apart from the Palais de Princes the visit includes the horrific oubliette dungeons which were really nothing more than pits below an opening in the dungeon floor through which prisoners were thrown down and left in the dark to rot. The tour ends at the museum which includes archaeological discoveries as well as items of local interest, documents and an extremely long panoramic view of the battle of 1870.

Although Sedan's other attractions cannot really compare with the fortress there are a few additional places that are also worth seeing. For example, the Église St-Charles, on the nearby Place d'Armes, was built as a Protestant church in the late sixteenth century but was handed over later to the Catholics, since when it has carried out the functions of a cathedral. From here the Place de la Halle leads directly to the Rue du Ménil with its fringe of old houses, the most historic being number 1, the Maison des Gros Chiens, which started out as a military academy but eventually became a royal factory producing an up-market variety of woollen fabrics. A short distance away, down the Avenue de Verdun, the Jardin Botanique is small but most attractive with some beautiful roses and a charming old-world atmosphere. On the opposite side of the Avenue de Verdun, behind a little church where the Vicomte de Turenne's parents and other princes of Sedan are buried, the Quai de la Regente is a pleasant promenade along the river with a view across to the Port de Plaisance and a small camping area.

Elsewhere in the town, beyond the old seventeenth-century Hôtel de Ville on the Rue de l'Horloge, one of the most elderly streets in Sedan, is the Place Turenne watched over by a statue of the famous vicomte. On the far side of the river is the Ancien Sous-Prefecture where Napoléon III dossed down for three nights during the Franco-Prussian War while, back on the opposite bank, on the Boulevard Gambetta, is the Tapis Point de Sedan factory. This turns out carpets of a very high standard that are exported all over the world and is open to visitors by appointment during working hours.

Sedan has nothing out of the ordinary in the way of hotels but the restaurant Au Bon Vieux Temps, in the Place de la Halle, is well known for its specialities, ranging from *langoustine* to venison when it is in season. However it is possible to find a bed and bath en suite for the night in order to inspect one or two other places in the vicinity. Among them probably the most emotive is the **Fort de la Ferté** that once marked the end of the Maginot Line. It withstood 4 days of continuous German attacks in May 1940 and was only captured after all the 105 defenders had either been killed or fatally wounded. **Bazeilles**, to the south-east, put up an equally determined fight in September 1870. The Maison de la Dernière Cartouche (House of the Last Cartridge), so-called because it was apparently the place where the last shot was fired, is given over almost completely to the history of the battle, along with items recovered from the ruins of numerous houses that were destroyed. The Château de Bazeilles, built by a rich wool manufacturer in 1750, would appear to have got off comparatively lightly. It is now a hotel complete with its original decorative windows and a restaurant in the orangery.

Mouzon, further south on the D964, has come a long way since it started life as a Roman outpost. Its centrepiece is the Gothic abbey church of Notre-Dame which originated in the twelfth century but was added to and adapted at intervals during the next 400 years. It has an intricately carved main door, an impressive nave and an eighteenth-century organ that plays its full part in the Autumn Festival. The village also contains a few old buildings known as the Spanish houses. There does not seem to be anything foreign about them so the name may simply mean that they survived a siege by Spanish forces in 1650. At that time Mouzon was fortified but the fifteenth-century walls were demolished a few years later and all that remains of them nowadays is the ancient Porte de Bourgogne. The village has always been industrially minded and its Musée du Feutre is concerned exclusively with felt. It not only demonstrates how the material is created from wool but also shows a host of different articles manufactured from it afterwards. Nothing is over-looked, from the type of cloaks worn by nomads in Turkey and Afghanistan to the part it plays in industry, not forgetting its role in fashion as well as in the production of toys and various kinds of decorations.

South of Mouzon, and reached by way of the D19 to Beaumont-en-Argonne and then along the D4, the **Belval-Bois-des-Dames** is an area that once belong to the local Augustine monks but has now been set aside as a special animal park. It has a road of sorts through the middle, footpaths through the woods, round the ponds and across the meadows and observation platforms at strategic intervals. All kinds of animals such as wild boar, moose, bison, various types of deer, bears and wild sheep roam about the large enclosures in comparative freedom. One of the most interesting things about this park is that it contains some species whose ancestors were living in the area anything from 1,500 to 2,000 years ago. From here there is a choice of routes leading northwards, back to Charleville-Mézières, or across to **Rethel** on both the N51 and the River Aisne as well as the Ardennes Canal.

Although Rethel had a lot to put up with during World War II, it still has the twelfth-century Église St-Nicolas, which was once at-tached to a Benedictine priory and needed a certain amount of restoration at the end of the War in Europe. Its main interest lies in the double nave and the fact that one of its figures is thought to have inspired the Coronation of the Virgin at Reims cathedral. The Musée du Rethelois et du Porcien dabbles in a whole range of subjects from archaeology and folklore to engravings and sacred art, but so far not a great deal of attention has been paid to the publisher, Louis

Hachette, who was born in Rethel nearly 200 years ago. All the three local hotels have restaurants and are in the two-star category, so it should not be too difficult to find a room if necessary before driving the last 39km (24 miles) to Reims in the morning.

AUBE

Aube, tucked away below Marne in the south-western corner of Champagne-Ardenne, is bordered by Aisne, Yonne and Burgundy's Côte d'Or. It is a tranquil *département* with its full share of lakes and forests as well as the inevitable vineyards, described in one official publication with poetic accuracy as 'champagne on the vine'. This *département* is not quite so well endowed with historic towns and villages as some of its neighbours but makes up for it with the Forêt d'Orient and the Forêt de Piney. Together they manage to provide an animal reserve and a bird sanctuary combined with extensive woodlands and a large man-made lake that already has a boating centre with, among other things, sailing lessons and organised excursions by motor launch.

❋   The main jewel in Aube's crown is unquestionably **Troyes**, the historic capital of Champagne. Its ancient heart, covering an area shaped like a champagne cork and partly enclosed by the River Seine, is full of splendid town houses, churches and museums. It is very well placed for motorists, being only 162km (100 miles) from Paris on the N19, 120km (74 miles) from Reims and only 77km (48 miles) from Châlons-sur-Marne. Once there the visitor has a whole range of hotels to choose from such as the Grand Hotel on the Avenue Maréchal Joffre, ☎ 25 79 90 90 or the slightly more convenient Hôtel de la Poste on the Rue Emile Zola, ☎ 25 73 05 05. Further down the scale is the delightful Motel Savinien, less than 10 minutes drive away in the Rue Jean de la Fontaine, just off the N60 at Ste-Savine, ☎ 25 79 24 90. It makes ample provision for swimmers, tennis players and disabled guests although there are one or two steps up to the restaurant which could prove awkward for anyone in a wheelchair. There is also a Youth Hostel at Rosières, south-west of Troyes, ☎ 25 82 00 65 and a two-star camp site on the northern outskirts of the city.

Troyes has had a long and somewhat chequered history since the days when it was a Gallo-Roman fortress called *Augustobona Tricassium*. It attracted the attention of Attila the Hun in AD451 but escaped the consequences when St-Loup, who was the resident bishop at the time, persuaded him that no useful purpose would be served by sacking it. Nothing of any great interest happened after that until the Normans burned the whole place down in AD889.

In due course the town passed into the hands of the Comtes de Champagne who spent a great deal of time and money turning it into a worthy capital. The great Talmudic scholar Salomon Rachi was a member of its influential Jewish community, the constitution of the Order of the Knights Templar was approved by the local Synod and merchants from far and near were attracted to its famous fairs. Eventually Champagne was united with France when the Countess Jeanne married Philippe le Bel, but in 1420 the Treaty of Troyes was signed, making Henry V of England heir to the throne when he married Catherine of France in the Église St-Jean-au-Marché in the city. Nine years later Troyes was liberated by Joan of Arc at the start of a victorious campaign that put an end to all Henry's carefully laid plans. A fire in 1524 once again destroyed a great deal of the city but much of the reconstruction work undertaken at that time survived the Wars of Religion, the Revolution and World War I, but was sadly battered about during World War II. However it picked itself up again, added new industries to its long list of traditional crafts, restored the majority of its ancient buildings and re-established itself as an important historical centre.

Guided tours of the city are available, either at set times or by special arrangement, but for people who prefer to do their sightseeing individually and at their own speed, it is a little difficult to know where to begin. There are, for example, nine different churches, all of them worth seeing, at least half as many museums and an abundance of splendid sixteenth-century mansions, picturesque little streets and elegant squares. Perhaps the easiest and most obvious first choice would be the Cathédrale St-Pierre-et-St-Paul, in the Place St-Pierre, on a site which had been occupied by two previous churches. Work began on the present building in 1208 and, although it was consecrated in 1430, went on more or less constantly for another 200 years. It has a typically Gothic façade dominated by a lofty tower, a beautiful rose window and plenty of intricate stone carving, but lost most of its statues in the Revolution. The interior is memorable for its size and elegance rather than its contents, the most valuable of which are kept in the treasury. They range from an eleventh-century casket to a collection of enamels, prayer books and alms boxes, many of which belonged to the Comtes de Champagne.

On one side of the cathedral is the Musée d'Art Moderne, housed in the former bishops' palace and separated by a courtyard containing two special trees. Nobody seems to know very much about the chestnut but the lime tree was grown from a cutting brought back from the Vatican in 1870. The art works on display in the museum include sculptures, ceramics and glass as well as drawings and paintings by such famous artists as Picasso, Degas, Cézanne, Gauguin, Pissaro and Toulouse-Lautrec. There are views of London, curious abstract canvasses and a section devoted to African art.

On the opposite side of the cathedral is the Musée St-Loup. This is really three museums for the price of one, occupying most of the former Abbaye St-Loup, built in the seventeenth century but adapted to present day needs. The Musée d'Histoire Naturelle on the ground floor has a splendid collection of birds from all over the world as well as a nice line in meteorites, leaving the Musée des Beaux-Arts et d'Archéologie to concentrate on antiquated discoveries that were made locally. Apart from its prehistoric exhibits there is a large bronze statue of Apollo left behind by the Romans, jewellery and arms from a tomb that was apparently overlooked by Attila, and medieval sculptures, many of them apparently from long-forgotten churches. The first floor is more of a picture gallery spanning some 500 years, with the addition of tapestries, sculptures and furniture. Among the famous artists who are represented are such well-known painters as Van Dyck, Rubens, Watteau and Fragonard. The third occupant of the building is the Bibliothèque, founded in 1651 since when it has collected not far short of half a million precious books and manuscripts. Several of its prize possessions came from abbeys and monasteries when they were pillaged during the Revolution.

Two quite sizeable blocks away along the Rue de la Cité, the Hôtel Dieu, that was once a hospital, faces the water across the Quai des Comtes de Champagne. This is a veritable magnet for hypochondriacs because it contains one of the most splendid old pharmacies to be found anywhere. The shelves, reached when necessary by using an enormous mobile step ladder, are weighed down with hundreds of painted wooden caskets designed to hold medieval herbs. There are nearly as many decorative porcelain bottles for liquid concoctions, as well as plates, jugs and jars, all kinds of pewter ware, documents and some sixteenth-century reliquary busts, presumably for patients who did not survive the cures. The hospital was founded in the twelfth century but was updated later when it was given a new chapel, a sundial and a gilt wrought-iron railing to separate the courtyard from the Rue de la Cité.

Across the water, in the Place de la Liberation, the Basilique St-Urbain is a perfect example of Gothic art in the thirteenth century. It owes its existence to Pope Urbain IV and was built on the site of his father's modest cobblers shop where he was born in 1185. It has of course been renovated, most recently in the nineteenth century when the west façade was added, but the tympanum over the main door with its carvings of the Last Judgement and the Resurrection of the Dead is the original. The interior fulfils every expectation, especially when the sunlight is pouring through the large thirteenth-century stained glass windows. Among its most arresting statues are St-Jean and the Vierge au Raisin whose very mature-looking Child seems to be unaware of the bird that is helping itself to their bunch of grapes. The remains of Pope Urbain were brought back to Troyes in 1901 and placed behind a plaque in the choir.

Other churches quite close by include the Église St-Rémy with its wooden spire and four bell turrets overlooking the Place St-Rémi and the large covered market across the road. The historic Église St-Jean, in the pedestrian precinct near the Rue Roger Salengro, has changed quite considerably since Henry V and Catherine were married there. It was severely damaged as a result of a serious fire about a hundred years later. The church with its oddly shaped clock tower, known as the Minaret, is of particular interest to Canadian visitors because Marguerite Bourgeoys, who founded the Congregation of Notre-Dame of Canada in Montreal, was baptised there in 1620.

The surrounding pedestrian area, called the Quartier St-Jean, is both fascinating and photogenic. The tiny, narrow streets are paved with cobbles as they were in the olden days, the splendid 400-year-old houses have been meticulously restored and only an occasional sign, and shop windows filled with present day merchandise, detract from the atmosphere. The most spectacular houses to look out for are the Maison du Boulanger, which has switched its allegiance from bread to champagne, the Maison de l'Orfèvre opposite, flaunting its round Goldsmith Turret, and the Hôtel Juvenal des Ursins on the Rue Champeaux which has a three-sided chapel built in 1526. Although the Rue Champeaux is wider than most, having been a main thoroughfare in the Middle Ages, the Ruelle des Chats is by far the most picturesque. There is plenty of room for two cats to pass each other, and even for two pedestrians if they are careful not to stand in the middle admiring the upper floors of the houses on either side that jut out until they almost meet overhead.

The area round about is also steeped in history. For example, Ruelle des Chats joins the Rue Charbonnet practically opposite the Rue de la Madeleine, which in turn leads to the twelfth-century Église Ste-Madeleine, the oldest church in Troyes. Its most outstanding attribute is the magnificently carved roodloft, one of the very few left in France, with its triple arches and a variety of attendant statues. The stained glass windows, dealing with such diverse subjects as the

The sixteenth-century Goldsmith Turret and the Maison du Boulanger in the pedestrian precinct, Troyes

The gilded entrance added in 1760 to the ancient Hôtel Dieu, Troyes

creation of the world, the Tree of Jesse and what looks like a pair of artisans at work, and the statue of Ste-Marthe at the foot of a pillar opposite the roodloft, also date from the early sixteenth century.

On the other hand, the Rue Général Saussier, leading off the Rue Emile Zola near the opposite end of the Ruelle des Chats, was once closely associated with the Knights Templar. Among the many atmospheric old houses in this area is the Hôtel de Mauroy, in the Rue de la Trinité, easily distinguished by its octagonal half-timbered turret. It started life as a hospital in the mid-seventeenth century, went on to become an orphanage and then got involved in the local hosiery industry when the children were put to work weaving stockings. In 1966 the building was taken over by an association of craftsmen who turned it into a museum of handicrafts, fitting it out with all the tools used by carpenters and other woodworkers as well as stone masons, metal workers and people involved in the leather industry. In addition it has an extensive library devoted to a wide range of skills and crafts and claims to be the only museum of its kind in the country.

A short distance away, in the Rue de Vauluisant, the sixteenth-century Hôtel de Vauluisant is occupied by the Musée Historique de Troyes et de Champagne and the Musée de la Bonneterie which specialises in hosiery. The building itself is most impressive with its two curved stone staircases leading up on either side of the main door between matching round turrets, each topped by a pointed roof like a dunce's cap overlaid with slates. The Museum of Troyes and Champagne is fairly predictable, full of statues and stonework, objects d'art, costumes and documents relating to the history of the city, whereas the Hosiery Museum is said to be unique. Apart from the ancient looms and other pieces of relevant equipment, there are superb examples of the various articles that were turned out locally over a period of more than 300 years. The exhibits, which literally run into thousands, include bags and gloves, slippers and embroidered stockings. The workmanship is really beautiful and partly explains why the trend-setters of the late nineteenth century were so anxious to show off their feet and ankles.

Within a stone's throw of these two museums the Église St- Pantaléon was built on the site of an ancient wooden church in the latter part of the sixteenth century. It has quite a few stained glass windows and is rather overburdened with statues, many of them installed at about the same time. The figure of St-Jacques is thought to have been created by Dominique le Florentin in his own likeness, but it is quite overshadowed by the highly coloured tableau showing the arrest of St-Crépin and Ste-Crépinien, carved by François Gentil for the Shoemakers Guild. Gentil was also responsible for a number of statues, including David and Isaiah, in the Église St-Nicolas, up the road apiece beyond the Place Jean Jaurès. One interesting feature of this church is the wide staircase leading to an open arcade above the nave which provided an upper entrance for the congregation in the days when the building was partly enclosed by the city walls. It also has some rather unusual stained glass windows and a full compliment of statues.

Having exhausted the many possibilities afforded by its churches and museums, Troyes still has plenty of other things to interest and entertain visitors who are prepared to look for them. There are two theatres, the Madeleine and the Champagne, memorials to the men who died in the Franco-Prussian War and to members of the Resistance who opposed Hitler, and the Argence Fountain, all within striking distance of the Boulevard Gambetta. A suitably restrained seventeenth-century Hôtel de Ville overlooks the Place Maréchal Foch, while almost every street in the old city has at least one decorative mansion left over from the past. In addition there is a skating rink in the Parc des Expositions, two swimming pools, a leisure centre and the not particularly convenient 18-hole Château de la Cordelière golf course which it shares with Chaource, 31km (19 miles) to the south.

Chaource is known principally for the quality of its cheese, but in addition to this there is an exceptionally fine *mise au tombeau* in the Église St-Jean-Baptiste which shows the Virgin Mary and her female companions dressed in the type of clothes worn by serving women in the sixteenth century. Also worth more than a passing glance is the colourful Nativity scene in one of the chapels, consisting of twenty or more moveable figures including the Three Wise Men and the shepherds. A few kilometres down the road, **Maisons-les-Chaource** has both a museum of antique dolls and the possibility of finding a bed for the night as well as some traditional cooking at the Hôtel-Restaurant aux Maisons which is one of the Logis de France.

From Chaource the D443 heads for **Bar-sur-Seine**, an attractive, elongated village that occupies both banks of the river in the shadow of a medieval castle. It is full of typical sixteenth-century buildings such as the Apothecary's House, and invites sightseers to inspect the stained glass windows and alabaster carvings in the Église St-Étienne. It has its own *logi* — the Hôtel-Restaurant le Barséquanais — which is popular with trout fishermen, who have at least three different streams to choose from, and with visitors who want to explore the surrounding area. Among the places to visit in the vicinity is **Essoyes** which appears in several Renoir paintings. He lived in the village for quite some time and is buried in the local churchyard with his sons Pierre and Jean. Then there is **Mussy-sur-Seine**, on the N71 just at the point where it crosses into the Côte d'Or on the way to Dijon. It has a château that has been taken over by the Mairie, a Resistance Museum consisting mainly of items connected with the local maquis in 1944 and the fifteenth-century Église St-Pierre-ès-Liens whose statues were added over the next 200 years.

To the north of the A5 autoroute connecting Troyes with Dijon, **Bar-sur-Aube**, on the N19, is another atmospheric little village that was a famous market town in medieval days. Its twelfth-century Église St-Pierre is surrounded by covered wooden galleries, added about 400 years later, where visiting merchants took cover during the famous Champagne Fairs. Other attractions include the Église St-Maclou that was once the private chapel of the Comtes de Bar, and the Chapelle Ste-Germaine, 4km (2 miles) to the south-west, dedicated to the saint who was martyred there by the Vandals in AD407 and consequently became a place of pilgrimage.

Anyone who is spending a weekend in this part of the country in July or August should make a point of visiting **Clairvaux**, south-east of Bar-sur-Aube on the D396. It was here that St-Bernard founded an abbey in 1115 that was the forerunner of more than 200 other Cistercian monasteries established throughout Europe before he died. It became rich and powerful and so, naturally, attracted the attention of Napoléon who ordered his followers to get rid of the monks and turn the eighteenth-century buildings into a prison. Some of them are open to the public but the main attraction is the Bernard de Clairvaux Pageant on Friday and Saturday evenings in the summer. It takes place in the open air and consists of fifteen tableaux recalling the major episodes of his life, with professional and amateur performers, horsemen, music, coloured lights and hundreds of authentic costumes, designed especially for the pageant.

Brienne-le-Château, also on the D396 but in the opposite direction, is even more closely tied up with Napoléon. He was sent to the local military academy at the age of 9 and as a result always had a soft spot for the town, particularly as it was also where he defeated Blücher in January 1814. These and other events in the life of the corporal-turned-emperor are adequately covered in the town's Musée Napoléon, housed in the original academy. The château once belonged to Jean de Brienne, the crusader whose family rose to equally giddy heights by producing one Emperor of Constantinople and two Kings of Jerusalem. The château is not open to visitors. Two remaining places to visit are the splendid thirteenth-century covered

Bar-sur-Seine; the old entrance gate to the town

The main bridge over the River Ource at Essoyes

market and a slightly younger church that was added to later, at regular intervals, with an assortment of fonts and iron grilles.

The **Forêt d'Orient**, south of Brienne-le-Château and east of Troyes, is an extensive natural park with a vast man-made lake in the middle that was built to control the waters of the Seine. Its functions are many and varied, and include such things as maintaining a bird sanctuary, protecting plants and animals and providing facilities for sailing and boating and organising excursions by motor launch from Mesnil-St-Père. This is a pleasant little resort with a beach and a small hotel, called the Auberge du Lac, which arranges sailing regattas during the season. The Maison du Parc, in the section known as the

The abbey at Clairvaux, founded by St Bernard, with its eighteenth-century monastery buildings

Forêt de Piney, is a typical farmhouse and the correct place to go for any additional information. **Piney** itself, on the D960, has some attractive old houses and a covered market to match, as well as the Hôtel-Restaurant le Tadorne in the Place de la Halle. On the other hand, **Géraudot**, a good deal closer to the water's edge, has an antiquated church, a beach, a modest hotel and three camp sites, the best of them being the Camping Départemental de l'Épine aux Moines.

Vendeuvre-sur-Barse, at the opposite end of the lake on the N19, goes one better than its neighbours with the remains of a sixteenth-century castle that makes an ideal setting for a *son et lumière* performance organised by the inhabitants for the sheer fun of taking part in it. From here it is only a short run back to Troyes or 42km (26 miles) to Chaumont, in Haute-Marne, to the east.

HAUTE-MARNE

A certain young Frenchman, fed up and far from home, once described Haute-Marne as a beautiful island floating in a sea of wine. This is not as fanciful as it sounds. The *département* has the champagne vineyards of Marne and Aube to the north and west, faces the famous Route du Vin in Alsace across the mountains of the Vosges and rests its feet on Burgundy's Côte d'Or. It is also extremely versatile, sharing water sports on the vast Lac du Der-Chantecoq with the *département* of Marne, covering its high ground with a patchwork quilt of fields and forests and giving rise to streams that grow into rivers like the Aube, the Marne and the Meuse before they reach the sea. In addition to a generous sprinkling of fortified towns and historic churches it has an ancient spa, places associated with famous men like Voltaire and Charles de Gaulle, a stud farm that welcomes visitors, a National College of Basketmaking and a cutlery industry turning out such things as scissors and surgical instruments.

There are plenty of major roads linking Haute-Marne with its various neighbours whose main towns, such as Nancy, Metz, Troyes, Reims, Auxerre and Dijon are less than 161km (100 miles) away. Paris and Strasbourg, Lausanne and Calais are all within comfortable driving distance while the *autoroute* heads down to Lyon on its way to the Mediterranean. Hotels are plentiful and cover a fairly wide range, most of them being quite acceptable without actually getting into the luxury bracket. In addition there are a handful of three and four-star camp sites, several less up-market ones, a good many *gîtes*, and *auberges* that make a point of catering for young travellers, mainly in Chaumont and St-Dizier. The *département* does not make a great song and dance about its traditional cooking but quietly points out that the vineyards at Coiffy-le-Haut, south of Bourbonne-les-Bains, have been replanted and are now producing both red and white wines.

St-Dizier, the northernmost town in Haute-Marne, is frankly industrial but despite all its new buildings has managed to retain a few unobtrusive links with the past. These include the Holy Ghost Tower in what remains of the ramparts, the church of Notre-Dame in the Rue Giros which was rebuilt in 1775, the sixteenth-century Église St-Martin-de-la-Noue and a few bits and pieces in the municipal museum. At the same time it has two comfortable hotels, the Gambetta on the Rue Gambetta, ☎ 25 56 52 10 and the Soleil d'Or on the Route de Bar-le-Duc, ☎ 25 05 68 22, and is conveniently close to the Lac de Der-Chantecoq with its organised trips by motor launch and facilities for various water sports.

The first item of interest south of St-Dizier is the Menhir de la Haute-Borne at **Fontaines-sur-Marne**, just off the N67 to the left. This megalith, which is almost 7m (23ft) high, is roughly 4,000 years old and attracted so much attention in the eighteenth century that it toppled over as a result of all the excavations that were carried out and had to be restored to its upright position in 1845. A touch further away in the opposite direction along the D9, where it meets the D2 from St-Dizier, the little town of **Wassy** manages to combine industry with history. It was here in 1652 that the Catholic followers of François de Guise stormed their way into the large barn and massacred all the Protestants who had gathered inside for a service, thereby sparking off the Wars of Religion. The Église Notre-Dame is considerably older and demonstrates the fact with a Roman tower and a Gothic doorway, whereas the Hôtel de Ville, complete with its astronomic clock, is only just over 200 years old.

All this contrasts sharply with the main attraction at **Montier-en-Der**, 14km (9 miles) away along the D4 at the point where it joins the D384. This is the home of the National Stud, founded by imperial decree in 1810 in the grounds of the old abbey. It is a large complex of stables, harness rooms and coach houses where horse races and other equestrian events are held every Thursday afternoon in the autumn. The town grew up round a seventh-century monastery built by the Benedictine monks in the Forêt du Der, which is the Gallic word for oak. Part of the buildings are still standing and so is the abbey church of St-Pierre-et-St Paul which was damaged by war on several occasions, most recently during a German bombardment in June 1940. The restored sections are most impressive with their lofty arches and nineteenth-century stained glass windows, especially when they are floodlit in the evenings.

For anyone with only a passing interest in horses the D4 from Wassy also provides a link with **Joinville** to the east on the N67. The village, watched over by a feudal castle built in 1546 by Claude de Lorraine, is best known for its Grand Jardin. This was designed by the original owner for his wife and is laid out in the style of Fontainebleau with exotic trees and sculptures, many of them the work of Dominique Florentine. *Son-et-lumière* performances are held there during the summer in addition to concerts and exhibitions of various descriptions. The Église Notre-Dame had to be rebuilt after a fire in the sixteenth century when it was presented with the rather fine Saint Sépulcre after the vaults had been restored.

Unfortunately the two most popular excursions from Joinville lie in opposite directions. Les Lancets de Melaire, as its name implies, is a road consisting almost entirely of hairpin bends through the area known as La Petite Suisse. There are marked footpaths for a stroll through the woods, rivers full of fish and the very viewable little Église St-Aignan at Poissons on the D427. By leaving Joinville on the D960 and returning via Poissons, the whole route only covers about 20km (12 miles). **Cirey-sur-Blaise** is a bit further away to the west, below Doulevant-le-Château on the D2. The local castle belonged to the Marquise du Châtelet, Voltaire's 'Divine Emilie', and he spent a considerable amount of time there between 1733 and 1749 before he discovered that she was two-timing him with the poet Saint-Lambert. A tour of the château, which is only open to visitors on summer afternoons, includes the library and reception rooms hung with tapestries as well as the little theatre which was opened by Voltaire when he was not too busy writing or designing the carving for the main door.

Many people feel that a visit to this part of Haute-Marne would not be complete without calling in at **Colombey-les-Deux-Églises**, a

The countryside around Colombey-les-Deux-Églises

small village on the N19 north-west of Chaumont, that would probably have gone unnoticed if President de Gaulle had not had his country home there. As it is, the hamlet is dominated by an enormous pink granite Cross of Lorraine erected in 1972 as a memorial to the famous wartime leader who adopted it as the emblem of the Free French forces during the War in Europe. He retired from public life in 1969, died at home the following year and was buried in the little country churchyard where his grave soon became a place of pilgrimage for thousands of his followers. Part of the family home, La Boisserie, is open to visitors including a salon filled with photographs and other souvenirs, the dining room and the library.

Chaumont, 23km (14 miles) away and known in its youth as Calvus Mons, was the country seat of the Comtes de Champagne for a brief period during the early thirteenth century. It still has an ancient keep, the Tour Hautefeuille, that was added to the fortress more than 200 years later. It is a picturesque small town built on an escarpment, with narrow streets full of antiquated houses, some with carved doors or turrets, and an immense viaduct built towards the end of the nineteenth century. The Basilique St-Jean-Baptiste, on the Rue St-Jean, is part Gothic and part Renaissance and contains a

The most outstanding landmark at Chaumont is the viaduct, with its fifty arches spanning the valley of the Suize

sixteenth-century Tree of Jesse, but its prize possession is an exceptionally realistic *mise au tombeau*. It shows ten figures grouped round the body of Christ, who, unlike most sculptures of the sepulchre, has already been placed in a shallow grave. Meanwhile, the museum in the remains of the ancient castle has a fragment of the mausoleum created for the Duc de Guise by Dominique Frementin, a sarcophagus from the time of the Franks and a selection of paintings, drawings and sculptures. Of equal interest are some pieces of pearl embroidery, dolls and the kinds of things they would need in a doll's house and a display of eighteenth- and nineteenth-century cribs.

Chaumont has a selection of quite modest hotels, the highest rating going to the Terminus Reine in the Place du Général de Gaulle, ☎ 25 03 66 66, close to the railway and bus stations. It also recommends the Restaurant du Buffet de la Gare for traditional cooking and awards two stars to the Parc Ste-Marie camp site on the Rue des Tanneries. Among the outdoor attractions provided for visitors are tennis and riding, cycling and canoeing as well as guided tours into the surrounding forests with the possibility of seeing animals like stags, wild boar and different kinds of deer.

Nogent-en-Bassigny, 23km (14 miles) to the east, not far off the D417 on the D1, specialises in making cutlery and similar articles. These are displayed to advantage in both the official Cutlery Museum, which is essentially businesslike, and a large private collection that is more imaginative as far as tourists are concerned. The latter contains such things as mother-of-pearl manicure sets from its golden age, knives with tortoiseshell handles, delicate embroidery scissors, little pointed hats for extinguishing candles and sheep shears that were commonplace in the eighteenth century.

Sightseers who are interested in dolmens or Gallo-Roman remains will find plenty to keep them occupied south of Nogent-en-Bassigny in the vicinity of **Montigny-le-Roi**, a nice little place without anything particularly outstanding to offer. La Pierre Alot, close to an ancient Roman road through the Lardigny forest, is a large stone with a peculiar hollow which could have been made by centuries of rain or created specially in pagan times for its role in a religious ceremony. The Devil's Stone, in the Forest of Marsois, weighs 9 tons and apparently collapsed after too many people discovered that they could move it with one hand. However it is still said to rise up by itself at midnight on Christmas Eve to reveal a fabulous treasure hidden underneath and to swing round into a different position at very infrequent intervals.

Andilly-en-Bassigny, due south of Montigny-le-Roi, is not nearly so secretive about its past. As part of *Andematunum* it was the centre of a thriving agricultural community in the second century AD. However, when the Romans moved out it was occupied by the Franks who turned it into a burial ground and even left behind the sparse remains of a funeral pyre. Comparatively recent excavations have unearthed a whole range of objects such as mosaics, a marble bust, frescoes and old implements, the majority of which are on display in the museum built on the site. In addition there are traces of a Gallo-Roman villa and other buildings including thermal baths.

The Romans appear to have been even more enamoured with **Bourbonne-les-Bains**, on the far side of the *autoroute* on the D417. The only difference between the two places seems to be that, while Andilly-en-Bassigny appears to have been content to rest on its laurels and gently moulder away, Bourbonne-les-Bains persevered with its thermal springs and eventually emerged as a modern spa. As one would expect it has a fair sprinkling of smallish hotels, a three-star camp site and specialises in the treatment of rheumatism and fractures. Among its most vivid reminders of the past are likenesses of pagan gods such as Minerva and Venus, treasures recovered from an ancient cesspool, sculptures and an assortment of marble and bronze objects left behind by the early inhabitants. Other attractions include a modest museum, an arboretum and an adjacent wildlife park. In addition there are the remains of a fortress at Bourmont, destroyed by Mazarin in 1645, and a so-called wooden zoo at Prez-sous-Lafauche, created from the branches of trees by craftsmen in the local workshop.

Bourbonne-les-Bains is only 53km (33 miles) from Chaumont and has a direct link with Épinal and dozens of other worthwhile towns and villages in both Lorraine-Vosges and Alsace. However it would be a pity to leave Haute-Marne before exploring one or two other places of interest in the south of the *département*. This is easy to do by simply following a different route from Chaumont. Instead of opting for cutlery and dolmens in the south-east, the D65 makes a B-line for **Châteauvillain** to the south-west. It is a very restful little hamlet on the edge of a large forest with a deer park, the Porte Madame and an ancient tower left over from its medieval fortifications, a large seventeenth-century dovecote, a chapel with some early frescoes and an attractive eighteenth-century wash-house.

The village keeps in touch via the D65 with **Arc-en-Barrios** on the D3, where there is a much older and larger dovecote and, somewhat unexpectedly, the Hôtel-Restaurant du Château d'Arc in the Place Moreau, ☎ 25 02 57 57. It lists among its modest attributes an 1896 steam engine that used to run the old saw-mill but is now powered by an electric motor and an enormous stone case in the shape of an egg, originally used to store ice from the local pond.

Hidden away in magnificent woods to the south of the D20, near Rouvres-Arbot, is the much publicised but not really unique Cascade d'Etufs. The rivers and streams hereabouts are rich in calcium which gradually builds up to create what are described as petrified waterfalls. This cascade is generally agreed to be the most spectacular as the water flows over a perfectly structured natural staircase, not all that far downstream from the source of the Aub. Further along the road **Auberive** grew up round a Cistercian abbey founded by St-Bernard in 1136. A good deal of it was rebuilt in the eighteenth century and there are still the remains of the old cloister, a ruined chapel and a wrought iron gate fashioned by Jean Lamour who did such outstanding work for the Place Stanislas in Nancy. From here the D428 crosses the *autoroute* and joins the N74 just south of **Langres**.

In the distant past a tribe called the Lingons built their most important settlement on a rocky spur overlooking the surrounding plateau. Then, after the death of their chief, Néron, his successor Sabinus took refuge in a cave near the source of the Marne and left the stronghold to the tender mercies of the Romans. As it turned out they treated it with respect and even added some buildings of their own. On the other hand the Franks, who came after them, were quite willing to allow a succession of bishops to manage the affairs of the diocese of Langres, which had existed since the second century AD. The bishops' efforts met with varying degrees of success until, eventually, prosperity returned during the Middle Ages. The ramparts were strengthened at quite regular intervals, churches and houses were built or renovated and in due course Langres broke out of its ancient straight-jacket to add new suburbs and develop modern industries.

There is no doubt that the ramparts are the town's most enduring feature, covering a distance of more than 4km (2 miles) with seven fortified gateways and reinforced by twelve separate towers. In the olden days halberdier guards patrolled the walkways and the adjoining streets to guard against a surprise attack. Now their modern counterparts offer visitors an opportunity to take part in a torchlight reconstruction, made even more realistic by the addition of costumes, weapons and a special password. At the end of the tour everyone congregates in an elderly tavern to share a Friendship Cup.

Anyone who prefers to explore in daylight can simply follow a series of brown glazed tiles that mark the route from the seventeenth-century Porte des Moulins right round the ancient town. Things to see include the even older Henri IV gateway, the original military pigeon loft and two orientation tables with views across the Plateau de Langres, the Marne valley and the Vosges. The most antiquated attraction is the Gallo-Roman arch, incorporated into the ramparts during the Middle Ages and older than the nearby Porte de l'Hôtel de Ville by some 1,400 years.

Having had a bird's eye view of the ancient city with its narrow alleys, covered passageways and picturesque houses, a comparable series of ochre-coloured tiles point the way for visitors who would like to inspect them at ground level. It also begins at the Porte des Moulins which, with one or two other original gates, is the only way in or out of the former stronghold. It pauses at the Tour St-Ferjeux, built in the reign of Louis XI, passes two conveniently sited hotels and then heads for the Place Diderot. The square is named after Denis Diderot, the philosopher who was born in Langres in 1713, was the author of several important works including the *Encyclopedia* and was captured in a pensive mood by Bartholdi for his statue in the middle of the square. From here the signs point along the Rue du Grand-Cloître in order to include an eye-catching, half-timbered house, but it is much quicker to carry on along the Rue Leclerc to the cathedral.

The Cathédrale St-Mammès, which sets the scene for Langres, was built in the twelfth century and was described by Violette le Duc as the best monument ever constructed. This is a somewhat extravagant claim, especially as it was burned down on a number of

The statue of Denis Diderot, the philosopher who was born in Langres, stands in the square that is named after him

occasions and only received its classical façade and matching towers a little over 200 years ago. The interior with its lofty nave and solid pillars is refreshingly elegant and uncluttered, containing few decorations apart from two sixteenth-century tapestries, recalling the legend of the saint, and the Amoncourt chapel completed during the Renaissance. A fifteenth-century door from the south aisle leads to the competently restored thirteenth-century cloister, now occupied by the municipal library. The Salle du Trésor was plundered during the Revolution but managed to save its reliquary of the saint and a few other sacred items.

On the other side of the Rue Aubert there is a statue of Jeanne Mance of particular interest to Canadians because she was partly instrumental in founding Montreal. Just a stone's throw away the Musée St-Didier is chiefly concerned with Gallo-Roman relics and sculptures from the Middle Ages and the Renaissance, whereas the Musée du Breuil-de-St-Germain restricts itself to more recent matters and especially to Diderot and the painter and engraver Claude Gillot. The museum is housed in a former mansion within striking distance of the Porte de l'Hôtel de Ville on the far side of the Place de Verdun. One room is filled with articles that belonged to Denis Diderot, including documents and some sculptures, but considerably more space is allotted to Gillot. Also on display are works by other artists, pieces of eighteenth-century furniture, books and a collection of nineteenth-century cutlery.

The marked route continues along the base of the ramparts and up the Rue de la Tournette to visit a Renaissance mansion in the Rue Cardinal Morlot. It is one of the most attractive houses in the old city with decorative columns, some stone carving, a former kitchen in the basement and a small oratory. The last place to be visited is the thirteenth-century Église St-Martin in the Place Jenson, but once again a great deal of the original church was destroyed by fire and the façade along with the tower, inspired by an Italian campanile, is less than 300 years old. A few hotels are tucked away among the ancient buildings including the Grand Hôtel de l'Europe, ☎ 25 85 10 88, on the Rue Diderot. It is a sedate, stone-fronted building with some quite ordinary rooms overlooking the courtyard and a restaurant that offers good food at reasonable prices. It is a trifle surprising to find a space for campers inside the walls below the Tour d'Orval and the Tour de Navarre. They were both built in the sixteenth century to protect the southern approaches to the town and have a spiral ramp for taking guns up to the shooting platform and a terrace that was covered over when the Tour de Navarre was used as a powder magazine in 1821.

There are plenty of things for visitors to do and see in the surrounding area such as riding, cycling, walking or boating on one of the small lakes encased in forests a few kilometres away. Other nearby attractions include the Château de Pailly, 12km (7 miles) to the south-east, off the N74 on the D122. It is a rather sombre country residence built on the site of an ancient fortress in the late sixteenth century by Gaspard de Saulx Tavanne who went to war with François I and rose to the rank of marshal. However its looks belie the beautifully decorated rooms inside.

Fayl-Billot, on the N19 to the south-east, has been engaged in making all sorts of cane and wickerwork objects for about 300 years. The techniques for growing the special kinds of willows and canes required were introduced by a monk called St-Peregrin with results that would no doubt have exceeded all his expectations. Today there is a large willow plantation called the Sallicetum as well as a National Cane Weaving School and a permanent exhibition of everything from various luxury items and furniture of all descriptions to baskets designed for anyone from housewives to fishermen. Some of the local craftsmen are delighted to show visitors round their workshops and explain the finer points of this traditional cottage industry. A selection of the finished articles make useful souvenirs, especially if they are marked with the Fayl-Billot quality label. Down the road, beyond the village, the D460 makes its way northwards through Laferté, which has nothing particular to offer, crosses the D417 at Bourbonne-les-Bains and continues on into the Vosges mountains en route for Épinal.

Additional Information

Places to Visit

MARNE

Châlons-sur-Marne
Bibliothèque
Place Maréchal Foch
Open: mornings and afternoons.
Closed Sundays, Mondays and holidays.
☎ 26 68 54 44

Cathedral Treasure
In the cathedral. In order to view enquire at the Syndicat d'Initiative or at the presbytery.

Église Notre-Dame-en-Vaux
Place Monseigneur Tissier
Closed on Sunday afternoons.

Église St-Alpin
Place Maréchal Foch
If closed enquire at the presbytery, 1 Rue St-Alpin
☎ 26 64 18 30

Église-St-Loup
Rue des Martyrs-de-la-Résistance
Open: Tuesday afternoons during July and August.

Musée du Cloître de Notre-Dame-en-
  Vaux
Rue de Vaux
Open: mornings and afternoons.
Afternoons only on Sundays and
holidays. Closed Tuesdays, 1
January, 1 May, 1 November, 11
November and 25 December.

Musée Garinet
Rue Pasteur
Open: afternoons only. Closed
Tuesdays and holidays.
☎ 26 68 54 44

Musée Municipal
Open: afternoons only. Closed
Tuesdays and holidays.
☎ 26 68 54 44

Épernay
Jardin des Papillons
Avenue de Champagne
Open: mornings and afternoons
May to mid-October.
☎ 26 55 15 33

Mercier Cellars
Avenue de Champagne
Open: for guided tours April to
October. Closed on weekdays in
December, January and February.
☎ 26 54 75 26

Moët et Chandon Cellars
Open: for guided tours mornings
and afternoons. Closed Saturdays,
Sundays and holidays November
to April.
☎ 26 54 71 11

Musée Municipal
Avenue de Champagne
Open: mornings and afternoons
March to November. Closed
Tuesdays, holidays and the second
or third Sunday in September for
the Fête d'Épernay.
☎ 26 51 90 31

Fort de la Pompelle
9km (6 miles) south-east of Reims
Musée
Open: all day.
☎ 26 49 11 85

Giffaumont
La Grange aux Abeilles
Open: every afternoon in July and
August. Saturday, Sunday and
holiday afternoons April to June
and during September. Sunday
afternoons only in October.

Village-Musée de Ste-Marie-du-Lac-
  Nuisement
Open: every afternoon during July
and August. Saturday, Sunday and
holiday afternoons April to June
and during September.
☎ 26 72 36 33

Lac du Der-Chantecoq
Information available from the
Maison du Lac, Giffaumont-
Champaubert, 51290 St-Remy-en-
Bouzemont
☎ 26 72 62 80
Boat trips leave Giffaumont every
afternoon from mid-April to mid-
September.

Montagne de Reims
Parc Naturel Régional de la Montage
  de Reims
For information about the park
enquire from the Maison du Parc,
51160 Pourcy.
☎ 26 59 44 44

Reims
Ancien Collège des Jésuites
Rue Gambetta
Open: for guided tours 10am,
11am, 2pm, 3pm, 3.30pm and
4.45pm. Closed Tuesday mornings,
Saturdays, Sundays, 1 January, 1
May, 14 July, 1 November, 11
November and 25 December.
☎ 26 85 51 50

Champagne Cellars in Reims

Charles Heidsieck
Allée du Vignoble
Visits by appointment only.
☎ 26 36 03 03

Heidsieck and Monopole
Rue Coquebert
Visits by appointment only.
☎ 26 07 39 34 or 26 49 59 25

Lanson
Boulevard Lundy
Visit by appointment only
Monday to Friday.
☎ 26 78 50 50

Mumm
Rue du Champ de Mars
Open: 9-11am and 2-5pm March
to October. Closed weekdays
and holidays out of season.
☎ 26 49 59 70

Piper Heidsieck
Boulevard Henry Vasnier
Open: daily for tours by moving
car 9am-5.15pm May to September, 9-11.45am and 2-5.15pm
March and April, October and
November. 9-11.45am and 2-
5.15pm Thursday to Monday
December to February.
☎ 26 85 01 94

Pommery
Place du Général Gouraud
Open: mid-March to early
November. For opening days
and hours.
☎ 26 61 62 55

Ruinart
Rue des Crayères
Visits by appointment only.
☎ 26 85 40 29

Taittinger
Boulevard Victor Hugo
Film show and guided tour.
9.30am-1pm and 2-5.30pm
Monday to Friday. 9am-12noon
and 2-6pm weekends and
holidays March to November.
Weekdays only December to
February ☎ 26 85 45 35

Veuve Clicquot Ponsardin
Place des Droits de l'Homme
Visits by appointment only.
☎ 26 40 25 42

Basilique St-Rémi
Son et lumière 9.30pm Saturdays
July to September.

Cathédrale Notre-Dame
Guides available during the
summer.

*Centre Historique de l'Automobile
    Française*
Avenue Georges Clemenceau
Open: mornings and afternoons.
Closed during the week in January
and February.
☎ 26 82 83 81

Chapelle Foujita
Rue du Champ de Mars
Open: mornings and afternoons.
Closed Wednesdays and some-
times out of season.
☎ 26 47 28 44

Cryptoporticus
Open: afternoons mid-June to mid-
September except on 14 July.
Closed Mondays.
☎ 26 85 23 36

Église St-Jacques
Off the Rue de Vesle
Closed Mondays.

Musée-Hôtel Le Vergeur
Place du Forum
Open: for guided tours 2-6pm
daily. Closed Mondays, 1 January,
1 May, 14 July, 1 November and 25
December.

Musée St-Denis
Rue Libergier
Open: mornings and afternoons.
Closed Wednesdays January, 1
May, 14 July, 1 November, 11
November and 25 December.

Musée St-Rémi
Rue Simon
Open: 2-6.30pm weekdays. 2-7pm
Saturdays and Sundays. Closed on
certain holidays.
☎ 26 85 23 36

Palais du Tau
Beside the cathedral
Open: mornings and afternoons.
Closed 1 January, 1 May, 8 May, 1
November, 11 November and 25
December.
☎ 26 47 49 37

Planetarium et Horloge Astronomique
In the Ancien Collège des Jésuites
Demonstrations at 3.15pm and
4.30pm weekdays and Saturdays
July and August. Otherwise

3.15pm Saturdays and 2.15pm,
3.30pm, 4.45pm Sundays.
☎ 26 85 51 50

Salle de Guerre
In the technical college
Open: daily 10am-12noon and 2-
6pm. Closed Tuesdays, 1 May, 14
July, 1 November, 11 November
and 25 December.
☎ 26 47 28 44

Vitry-le-François
Église Notre-Dame
Closed on Sunday and holiday
afternoons.

ARDENNES
Bazeilles
Maison de la Dernière Cartouche
Open: mornings and afternoons.
Closed Fridays.

Belval-Bois-des-Dames
Parc de Vision
Open: every day during July and
August. Wednesdays, Saturdays,
Sundays and holidays in the
afternoon from February to June
and September to mid-October.
☎ 24 30 01 86

Charleville-Mézières
Musée Rimbaud
In Le Vieux Moulin
Open: mornings and afternoons.
Closed Mondays, 1 January and 25
December.
☎ 24 33 31 64

Chooz
Centrales Nucléaires des Ardennes
Open: for guided tours daily except
Sundays and holidays. It is wise to
arrange visits in advance.
☎ 24 42 05 26

Fort de la Ferté
Open: every afternoon during July
and August. Sunday and holiday

afternoons only Palm Sunday to June and September and October.
☎ 24 22 06 72

Givet
Grottes de Nichet
4km (2 miles) east of the town
Open: for guided tours mornings and afternoons April to September.
☎ 24 42 00 14

Forge Toussaint
On the Quai de Meuse
Open: for guided tours mornings and afternoons mid-June to mid-September.

Fort de Charlemont
Open: for guided tours mornings and afternoons July and August.

Tour Victoire
Near the Forge Toussaint
Open: for guided tours mornings and afternoons mid-June to mid-September.

Montcornet-en-Ardenne
Château
2km (1 mile) south-east of Renwez
Open: afternoons during July and August except on Mondays. Saturday and Sunday afternoons only from Easter to June and September to All Saints Day.
☎ 24 54 93 48

Monthermé
Église St-Léger
Open: on weekdays during July and August. At other times enquire by telephone, ☎ 24 53 08 74.

Mouzon
Musée du Feutre
Open: mornings and afternoons July and August. Afternoons only June and September. Saturday and Sunday afternoons only May and October.
☎ 24 26 10 63

Rethel
Église St-Nicolas
If closed enquire at the presbytery, 13 Rue Carnot
☎ 24 38 41 50

Revin
Galerie d'Art Contemporain
Open: Wednesday, Saturday and Sunday afternoons only.

Rocroi
Musée
In the Corps de Garde
Open: mornings and afternoons from Easter to September. Otherwise afternoons only.
☎ 24 54 24 46

Sedan
Château Fort
Open: for guided tours daily April to August, weekday afternoons except Mondays September to mid-November and all day on Sundays.
☎ 24 29 03 28

Warcq
Église
Enquire at the Mairie Monday to Saturday.

AUBE
Brienne-le-Château
Église
If it is closed enquire at the Mairie or from Monsieur le Curé, 94 Rue de l'Ecole Militaire ☎ 25 92 82 26

Musée Napoléon
Open: mornings and afternoons March to November. Closed Tuesdays and holidays.
☎ 25 92 82 41

Clairvaux
Abbaye
Guided tours at 1.45pm and 3.30pm on the first Saturday of each month from May to October and on the third Saturday in

September. Photography is forbidden and some form of identity may be required.

Essoyes
Maison de la Vigne et Souvenirs de Renoir
Open: 3-6pm Easter to All Saints Day, but throughout the day at weekends, holidays and from mid-June to mid-September.

Géraudot
If the church is closed enquire at 1 Rue du Général-Bertrand
☎ 25 41 24 21

Maisons-les-Chaource
Musée des Poupées d'Antan
Open: daily 9.30am-12noon and 2-6pm. Closed Tuesdays.

Mussy-sur-Seine
If the church is closed enquire at either 2 Rue des Ursulines
☎ 25 38 42 89 or
37 Rue Gambetta
☎ 25 38 43 33

Musée de la Résistance
Open: Saturday, Sunday and holiday afternoons May to October.
☎ 25 38 40 10

Orient
Lake and Forest
Maison du Parc
Open: mornings and afternoons daily. Closed 25 December and 1 January.
☎ 25 41 35 57

Parc de Vision de Giber
Open: Saturdays, Sundays and holidays at certain times from April to September. Otherwise on the first and third Sundays of each month. Trips round the lake from Mesnil-St-Père each afternoon from March to mid-September.
☎ 25 41 21 64

Troyes
Basilique St-Urbain
Place de la Libération
Open: all day from July to mid-September. At other times enquire at the Tourist Office or at 5 Rue Charbonnet.

Bibliothèque
In the former Abbaye St-Loup
Rue de la Cité
Open: 10am-12noon and 2-7pm. Closed Sundays and holidays.

Cathedral Treasure
Open: afternoons mid-June to mid-October. Closed Tuesdays, and Saturday and Sunday afternoons at Easter and on All Saints Day.

Église Ste-Madeleine
Open: mornings and afternoons from Easter to September. Otherwise enquire at the Tourist Office.
☎ 25 73 00 36

Église St-Jean
In the pedestrian precinct
Open: all day from July to mid-September. At other times enquire at the Tourist Office.

Église St-Nicolas
Near the Boulevard Victor Hugo
Open: every afternoon.

Église St-Pantaléon
On the Rue de Vauluisant and the Rue de Turenne
Open: during July and August. Otherwise enquire at the Tourist Office or at the presbytery.

Église St-Rémy
Enquire at the Tourist Office

Maison de l'Outil
Hôtel de Mauroy
Rue de la Trinité
Open: each morning and afternoon.
☎ 25 73 28 26

Musée d'Art Moderne
Place St-Pierre
Open: mornings and afternoons.
Closed Tuesdays, 1 January, Easter
Monday, 1 and 8 May, Ascension
Day, Whit Monday, 14 July, 15
August, 1 and 11 November and 25
December.

Musée de la Bonneterie
Hôtel de Vauluisant
Open: mornings and afternoons.
Closed Tuesdays and holidays.
☎ 25 73 49 49

*Musée Historique de Troyes et de
   Champagne*
Hôtel de Vauluisant
Rue de Vauluisant
Open: mornings and afternoons.
Closed Tuesdays and holidays.
☎ 25 73 49 49

Musée St-Loup
Rue Crestien de Troyes
Open: mornings and afternoons.
Closed Mondays and holidays.
☎ 25 73 49 49

Pharmacie de l'Hôtel-Dieu
Quai des Comtes de Champagne
Open: mornings and afternoons.
Closed Tuesdays and holidays.
☎ 25 73 49 49

N.B. Most of the museums, unless
otherwise stated, are open from
10am-12noon and 2-6pm. A
combined ticket is available for the
Musée des Beaux-Arts, the Hôtel-
Dieu and the Hôtel Vauluisant as
well as the Musée d'Art Moderne.

HAUTE-MARNE
Andilly-en-Bassigny
Gallo-Roman Remains
22km (14 miles) north-east on the D35
off the D74
Open: morning and afternoon from
Easter to end of August.

Chaumont
Musée Municipal
In the castle
Open: in the afternoons. Closed
Tuesdays and holidays.

Cirey-sur-Blaise
Château
Open: for guided tours afternoons
mid-June to mid-September.
Closed Tuesdays ☎ 25 55 43 04

Colombey-les-Deux-Églises
La Boisserie
Open: mornings and afternoons.
Closed Tuesdays ☎ 25 01 52 52

Fayl-Billot
To visit the workshops enquire
from the Tourist Office in Langres.

Joinville
Château du Grand-Jardin
Enquire from the Syndicat d'Initiative.

Langres
Église St-Martin
If closed ☎ 25 87 11 63

Musée du Breuil-de-St-Germain
Open: mornings and afternoons.
Closed Tuesdays, 1 January, 1 May,
1 November and 25 December.
☎ 25 87 08 05

Musée St-Didier
Enquire from the Tourist Office.

Tours de Navarre et d'Orval
Guided tours at 3pm Sundays and
holidays, 5pm Tuesdays and
Thursdays mid-June to mid-Sept
Also 8.30pm on Mondays in July.

Montier-en-Der
Haras National
Open: for guided tours afternoons.
☎ 25 04 22 17

Prez-sous-Lafauche
Zoo de Bois
Open: June to mid-September
afternoons. Closed Monday.
☎ 25 31 57 76

Wassy
Astronomic Clock
In the Hôtel de Ville
In order to see the clock enquire at
the Mairie on Monday to Friday.
☎ 25 55 31 90

Tourist Information Centres

Marne

Châlons-sur-Marne
Office de Tourisme
3 Quay des Arts
☎ 26 65 17 89

Épernay
Office de Tourisme
Avenue de Champagne
☎ 26 55 33 00

Giffaumont-Champaubert
Maison du Lac
☎ 26 72 62 80

Reims
Office de Tourisme et Accueil de
France
Rue Jadart
☎ 26 47 25 69

Ste-Menehould
Place du Général Leclerc
☎ 26 60 85 83

Vitry-le-François
Place Giraud
☎ 26 74 45 30

Ardennes

Charleville-Mézières
Office de Tourisme
Rue Mantoue
☎ 24 33 00 17

Revin
Bureau de Tourisme
Open: Easter to September
☎ 24 40 15 65

Mairie
☎ 24 40 10 44

Rocroi
Syndicat d'Initiative
Place Hardy
Open: Easter to September.
☎ 24 54 24 46

Sedan
Office de Tourisme
Place Crussy ☎ 24 29 31 14
and at the Fort (Palm Sunday to
late October) ☎ 24 27 22 93

Aube

Bar-sur-Aube
Syndicat d'Initiative
In the Hôtel de Ville
☎ 25 27 04 21

Troyes
Office de Tourisme and Accueil de
France
Boulevard Carnot
☎ 25 73 00 36

Quai Dampiere
Open: July to mid-September.
☎ 25 73 36 88

Haute-Marne

Bourbonne-les-Bains
Office de Tourisme
Place du Bains
Open: March to November.
☎ 25 90 01 71

Chaumont
Syndicat d'Initiative
Boulevard Thiers ☎ 25 03 04 74

Joinville
Syndicat d'Initiative
Rue Briand
Open: summer only ☎ 25 96 17 90

Langres
Office de Tourisme
Place Bel'Air ☎ 25 87 03 32

St-Dizier
Office de Tourisme
Pavillon du Jard ☎ 25 05 31 84

2

LORRAINE-VOSGES

The province of Lorraine consists of four *départements*. Those in the north, reading from left to right, are Meuse, Meurthe-et-Moselle and Moselle whereas Vosges, to the south, considers itself in some respects to be a separate entity. Certainly it is much more mountainous than the adjoining plateau and has lakes left over from the Ice Age, several different varieties of plants and wild life and is better equipped for agriculture and forestry than for mining and its attendant industries. Most of the mineral deposits are confined to the northern sector bordering on Belgium and Luxembourg, with iron predominating in Meuse and Meurthe-et-Moselle.

Lorraine's two most important cities are Metz and Nancy, followed by centres like Verdun and Thionville and a good many spas such as Vittel, Contrexéville and Plombières-les-Bains. The province is readily accessible by road, rail and air with regular flights to Metz and Nancy, both of which have motorail facilities for drivers who would rather do the first part of their journey to north-eastern France by train. Motorists who are in a hurry usually opt for one of the *autoroutes* and especially the A4 which connects Paris with Reims, bypasses Verdun and circles round Metz on its way to Strasbourg. Meanwhile the A31 *autoroute* is the quickest way to get from Thionville, on the Luxembourg border, to Metz and Nancy as well as Toul. In addition there are several major roads to choose from and a whole host of the smaller, frequently more attractive variety for anyone who plans to explore the surrounding area en route.

Historically Lorraine has something to offer even the most dedicated sightseer. Its attractions range from ancient forts and castles, impressive churches and little isolated chapels to the battlefields of Verdun and remnants of the Maginot Line. There are fascinating museums as well as craft workshops producing such things as

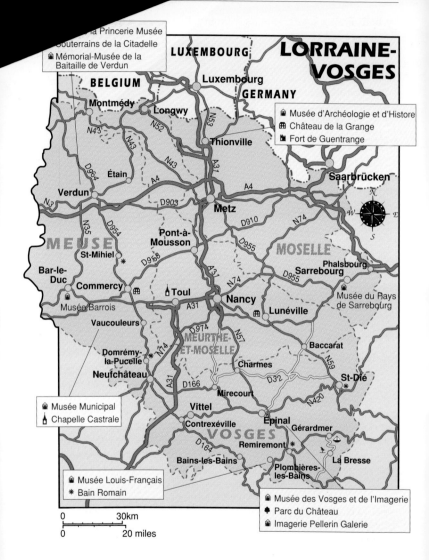

... la Princerie Musée
Souterrains de la Citadelle
Mémorial-Musée de la Bataille de Verdun

LUXEMBOURG

GERMANY

LORRAINE-VOSGES

BELGIUM

Luxembourg

Montmédy
Longwy

Musée d'Archéologie et d'Histoire
Château de la Grange
Fort de Guentrange

Thionville

Saarbrücken

Étain

Verdun

Metz

MEUSE

Pont-à-Mousson

MOSELLE

St-Mihiel

Bar-le-Duc

Commercy

Toul

Nancy

Phalsbourg
Sarrebourg

Musée Barrois

Lunéville

Musée du Pays de Sarrebourg

Vaucouleurs

MEURTHE-ET-MOSELLE

Baccarat

Domrémy-la-Pucelle

Charmes

St-Dié

Neufchâteau

Mirecourt

Musée Municipal
Chapelle Castrale

Vittel

Contrexéville

Épinal

Gérardmer

VOSGES

Remiremont

Bains-les-Bains

Plombières-les-Bains

La Bresse

Musée Louis-Français
Bain Romain

Musée des Vosges et de l'Imagerie
Parc du Château
Imagerie Pellerin Galerie

0   30km
0   20 miles

musical instruments or beautiful pieces of glass that make ideal
presents or souvenirs. In its early days Lorraine was fiercely independent, defending itself against repeated attempts at domination

by both France and Germany. The inhabitants were described as single-minded and determined by their friends, whereas their enemies were more inclined to use words like stubborn and pigheaded when talking about them. No-one, for example, could have been more determined than Joan of Arc who was born at Domrémy-la-Pucelle. More recently the distinctive Cross of Lorraine, traditionally associated with patriotism, became the symbol of the Free French under General de Gaulle during World War II.

Although Alsace has undoubtedly received more compliments down the ages for its food and wines, Lorraine has steadfastly refused to be left behind, making a feature of such things as Meuse crayfish, macaroons from Nancy and the widely-known egg-and-bacon tart called simply Quiche Lorraine. When it comes to entertainments the *département* more than holds its own. Daffodils predominate during the Fête de Jonquilles at Gérardmer in April, leaving Nancy to follow with its Theatre Festival in May, while Épinal's Festival International de l'Image is held in June. August is the time for a massive fireworks display at Gérardmer as well as performances at the Théâtre du Peuple at Bussang, said to be the oldest people's theatre in France, while Metz is kept busy making decorative floats for the Fête de Mirabelle at the end of the month. Between times there are organised excursions up into the mountains on horseback, opportunities for tennis, fishing, golf and water sports as well as gentle strolls or long-distance walks along any of the blazed footpaths.

There are plenty of places to stay in Lorraine to suit every type of budget. If money is reasonably plentiful, first class hotels can be found in most of the main centres, with a selection of up-market restaurants attached or in the immediate vicinity. However, visitors who have to watch their *francs* more carefully will find just as many small but perfectly adequate establishments in both towns and villages. In addition there is a network of *auberges* and *logis* which never drop below an official standard, often excel in local dishes and are almost invariably delightful. Finally, for people who prefer to cater for themselves, there is a certain amount of furnished accommodation on offer, either privately owned or part of a holiday village, as well as a variety of sites on which to pitch a tent or park a caravan.

MEUSE

It is by no means essential to have a good working knowledge of military matters in order to enjoy a visit to **Verdun**, but it certainly does help. The town, built on the hilly banks of the River Meuse and its attendant canals, has been a strategic centre since Roman times when it was a fortress known as *Virodunum Castrum*. Later, having been part of Charlemagne's Holy Roman Empire, it passed after his death into the hands of the rulers of Lorraine. In 1552 it was occupied by Henri II of France, was besieged on at least two subsequent occasions, from which it emerged battered but more or less intact, and by 1914 had become one of the most powerful fortresses in eastern France. However, early in 1916 the Germans attacked Verdun, anticipating an Allied offensive, and the fighting went on continuously for 10 months. The following year the French resumed their operations and within a few weeks had taken 10,000 prisoners and captured more than a hundred guns. By the time the war ended in 1918 the death toll on both sides was horrendous and the surrounding countryside bristles with cemeteries and monuments, covering an extremely wide area.

Despite its war-torn history Verdun has managed to preserve a few relics from the past, the most outstanding of them being the Cathédrale Notre-Dame on a hill overlooking the river. Admittedly it had to be rebuilt after a fire in 1048, and was updated and improved upon at intervals thereafter, but it still has a crypt dating from the twelfth century. The cloister was added some 400 years later, replacing an earlier one that had been demolished. Among the main things to look for are the beautifully decorated Portail du Lion and a variety of carved capitals, the most recent of which incorporate scenes from the battles that took place in 1916. The Palais Épiscopal, built next door in the eighteenth century, is equally eye-catching with its Court of Honour and some erstwhile apartments appropriated by the municipal library.

The Hôtel de la Princerie was originally the home of the most important local church dignitary apart from the bishop and has its own medieval cloister to emphasise the fact. However the building has now been taken over by the authorities and converted into the Musée Municipal with a finger in almost every pie. It starts with a prehistoric section and moves on to antiquities from Egypt, Greece and northern Italy before dealing with Gallo-Roman remains. The Middle Ages and the Renaissance are both well represented. Also on display are some quite nice pieces of furniture, pictures, weapons and early pottery. The museum is only about three blocks from the

cathedral on the Rue Belle-Vierge, near the Place Maginot, and e
closer to the Monument de la Victoire, commemorating the defe
of Verdun.

Within easy reach of the monument is the fourteenth-century
Porte Chaussée, guarding the eastern approach to the city over the
River Meuse. It consists of two sturdy round towers crowned with
battlements which, when there was no fighting to be done, came in
very handy as a prison. Its counterpart is the Porte Châtel, slightly
older and serving no particular purpose these days on the Rue
Mautroté at the entrance to a one-way street leading to the cathedral.
Beyond it is the vast Citadelle, standing on the site of the famous
Abbaye de St-Vanne, founded in AD952. The only remaining vestige
of the monastery is the Tour St-Vanne which Vauban preserved
when he refashioned the ancient fortress and strengthened the
ramparts. Below ground level are the Souterrains, some 7km (4
miles) of galleries, rooms and passages that provided shelter for the
defending army. The troops were self-sufficient within reason, even
down to a bank of ovens that could turn out more than 28,000 rations
of fresh bread by working round the clock.

Verdun also has a selection of small churches of no particular merit
and the remains of its southern fortifications enclosing little gardens
on either side of the Avenue d'Alsace-Lorraine. In addition, anyone
who plans to stay long enough to tour the battlefields will find two
comfortable hotels — the Bellevue on the Rond-point de Lattre-de-
Tassigny near the Parc des Sports, ☎ 29 84 39 41 and the Hostellerie
du Coq Hardi on the Avenue de la Victoire that runs beside the river,
☎ 29 86 36 36. The latter is quite atmospheric and has an excellent
restaurant. Neither could be described as cheap but there are some
smaller establishments for people who have to watch their *francs*
quite carefully.

The most frequently visited battlefields of World War I are to be
found in hilly country to the north-east about 5 to 10km (3 to 6 miles)
away. The site of each major engagement is marked by a cemetery,
a monument or, occasionally, a small museum. The most impressive
of these is the Mémorial-Musée de la Bataille de Verdun which
explains the various stages of the battle, augmented by uniforms,
weapons, pieces of military equipment and official documents of one
kind or another. Nearby are the ruins of a village and a small chapel
believed to be a replacement for the ancient church that once belonged to Fleury. Not far away, to the north-east, is the Fort de
Douaumont, parts of which have been carefully preserved, and the
enormous, rather Egyptian-looking Ossuaire de Douaumont, standing guard over an expanse of white crosses and deep red roses. The

The town of Verdun is threaded through by the River Meuse and its attendant canals

The Ossuaire de Douaumont and the graves of soldiers killed in World War I, Verdun

Ossuaire was built to the memory of nearly half a million French soldiers, has a small museum in the Tour des Morts and a view from the top of the tower from where it is possible to follow the course of the battle.

There are also a few reminders of World War II in the vicinity. Foremost among them are the memorial to Andre Maginot, the Minister of War who died in 1932, and an encounter in 1944 incorporated into the Monument des Fusillés, south of Vaux. A good deal further away, to the north-west, is the large American cemetery of **Romagne-sous-Montfaucon** with its 14,000 white marble tombstones. The battle itself is recalled by a monument commemorating the successful American First Army, built on the Butte de Montfaucon by the United States government with a great many steps leading up towards the Statue of Liberty.

Anyone whose interest in twentieth-century battlefields and their attendant cemeteries tends to evaporate before the day is out can plan quite different excursions from Verdun. One might well be northwards along the valley of the Meuse as far as Stenay on the D964. The only places with anything to offer en route are Dun-sur-Meuse, where there is a sixteenth-century church, and the tiny hamlet of **Mont-devant-Sassey** which started work on its local church more than 900 years ago. Later this was transformed into a fortress but fortunately the work did not encroach on the ancient crypt. It is unusually high with columns supporting the rounded arches and some quite attractive stone carving. **Stenay** itself was fortified by Vauban on the instructions of Louis XIV but nowadays it is more concerned with light industry. On the outskirts of the village a small museum, whose exhibits range from archaeology to local arts and crafts, has been set up in the house once occupied by the commander of the fortress.

From Stenay the D947 heads for **Montmédy**, 17km (11 miles) to the north-east. The town is divided into two sections, of which only Montmédy-Haut contains anything of interest to sightseers. It is, in reality, a small fortress that has had many owners in its lifetime, including Bourgogne, the Habsburgs and even the Spanish. It was returned to France in the seventeenth century when its defences were updated by Vauban. There is only one way in or out through the ramparts which enclose a few buildings including a small church, all huddled together on their isolated hilltop overlooking Montmédy-Bas and the surrounding countryside.

Avioth, on a small minor road 8km (5 miles) due north and within sight of the Belgian frontier, would hardly be worth worrying about if it were not for its magnificent basilica. This owes its existence to the discovery of a miraculous statue of the Virgin towards the end of the eleventh century, since when it has been the focal point for pilgrims. The church is beautifully decorated both inside and out with elaborately carved doorways, some fourteenth-century frescoes and a restored eighteenth-century organ. Facing the south door is the splendid little Recevresse, adjoining the entrance to what was once an ancient cemetery. It is like a miniature chapel where pilgrims in the olden days could leave their offerings for the Virgin.

The quickest way back to Verdun, 56km (35 miles) from Avioth, is through Montmédy and along the N43, pausing perhaps at **Louppy-sur-Loison** where the Renaissance château that once belonged to Simon de Pouilly, the governor of Stenay, is open to visitors. The road joins the N18 at Longuyon which carries on uneventfully to **Étain**, whose medieval church survived two World Wars, before making a right-hand turn on to the N3 for the last part of the journey.

An alternative option for a day out from Verdun would be to take the D964 in the opposite direction, southwards, in order to explore the Côtes de Meuse. It is a pleasant enough drive along the river valley to St-Mihiel, although a combination of the D904 and the D908 is longer but has more to offer along the way. **Hannonville-sous-les-Côtes**, for example, has a museum with a reconstructed vine-grower's house from the nineteenth century which is authentic in every respect. Further down the road **Hattonchâtel**, on the edge of the Forêt de la Montagne, has a nice old church and an ancient château that fell foul of Cardinal Richelieu in 1634. However the building was restored to something like its medieval stature in the 1920s and since then has been open to visitors. A little further on, through Vigneulles-les-Hattonchâtel, the D908 takes the long way round past the Lac de Madine. This is a popular leisure area, sadly lacking in hotels of any description but with a 9-hole golf course in the vicinity. The monument crowning the Butte de Montsec commemorates the 1918 September offensive by the American First Army and has a splendid view over the lake and the Côtes de Meuse.

There are several good reasons for visiting **St-Mihiel**, whether by taking a minor shortcut or carrying on to the D907. The town, strung out along the river banks, started life as a small community which grew up round the Benedictine Abbey of St-Mihiel, or St-Michel, founded in AD709. During the reign of Charlemagne one of his counsellors, who was also the resident abbot, transferred his domain to a spot a trifle closer to the river. Not a great deal of this building has survived apart from the church and the adjoining palace with its façade designed in the style of Louis XIV. The church has a Romanesque tower and a good many statues including the *Swooning Ma-*

donna by Ligier Richier who was a local resident. He was given the job of decorating the town for the visit of Charles III in 1559 but shortly afterwards he became a Protestant and went to live in Geneva where he died some 8 years later. Despite the excellence of his Madonna Richier surpassed this sculpture with *Le Sépulcre*, an intricately carved *mise au tombeau* in the Église St-Étienne, three or four blocks away, just off the Rue du Dr A. Thierry. The only other things to see are the Maison du Roi, a fourteenth-century mansion in the Rue Notre Dame that once belonged to René of Anjou, and a rocky outcrop known as the Falaises.

Commercy, 53km (33 miles) south of Verdun on the River Meuse, is a singularly uninspiring little place where even the château does not come up to expectations. This may be because it was badly damaged by fire in 1944 and appropriated later to serve as offices for the municipality. However there are conducted tours round some of the older parts of the building which was once a desirable residence belonging to Stanislas Leszczinski, the deposed king of Poland who was also ruler of Lorraine.

Vaucouleurs, beyond Void on the D964, is infinitely more rewarding. It was from here that Joan of Arc set out on her mission to save France from the English who had bedevilled her homeland for a hundred years. She persuaded the governor to provide her with a small company of soldiers and in February 1429 she led them out through the now rather dilapidated Porte de France to confront the Dauphin. The old archway still stands on the hillside overlooking the town, close to the ancient Chapelle Castrale, built over a thirteenth-century crypt where she prayed to the statue of Notre-Dame-des-Voûtes.

The château itself has all but disappeared above ground level, although it has been partly excavated by Henri Bataille who is usually on hand to show visitors round, explain all the finer points and invite them to inspect his miniscule museum. Just down the hill, on the Rue Jeanne d'Arc, the Hôtel de Ville has devoted one wing to the Musée Municipal. The exhibits are almost entirely concerned with local history and, of course, Joan of Arc. However there is also a bust of the Comtesse du Barry, the daughter of a local seamstress who went to Paris and set up home with Comte Jean du Barry who introduced her to Louis XV. She became the king's mistress in 1769 and for the remainder of his reign exerted considerable influence at court, making and unmaking ministers as the spirit moved her. She did not have the same success with Louis XVI but nevertheless followed him to the guillotine in December 1793. A little further down the road is a small eighteenth-century church with some quite viewable frescoes in the vaults.

From Vaucouleurs several options are open to motorists with the time and inclination to explore other *départements* in Lorraine-Vosges. Nancy, the most important city in Meurthe-et-Moselle, is 46km (29 miles) to the east whereas the spa tows of Contrexéville and Vittel are within easy reach of Neufchâteau on the far side of the border with the Vosges. Anyone heading north to Verdun can follow the D964 all the way, a distance of 73km (45 miles), or turn off along the N4 at Void in order to visit **Bar-le-Duc** on the N135.

This historic centre spreads itself across both the River Ornain and the Canal de la Marne au Rhin and has all the necessary ingredients to ensure its popularity with visitors. The Hotel Duc, Parc Bradfer, ☎ 29 79 32 66, is comfortable and has a reasonably-priced restaurant, there is a 9-hole golf course at Combles-en-Barrois 5km (3 miles) to the north-east and the old quarter, La Ville Haute, is memorable for its half-timbered houses and slightly younger decorative stone mansions.

Bar-le-Duc was founded by the Franks, became the capital of the local counts in AD954, was promoted to a dukedom 400 years later and provided headquarters for General Petain in its Château de Morbeaumont during World War I. All that remains of the original ducal palace is the Tour de l'Horloge, reached on foot from the Avenue du Château or, more conveniently, off the Rue du Baile beyond the Musée Barrois. The museum is housed in a Renaissance château that also belonged to the Ducs-de-Bar and covers a whole variety of different subjects. It takes a worldwide interest in ethnology, dabbles in natural science, preserves regional crafts and traditions and includes some not very inspiring pictures.

A block or two beyond the museum the road changes its name to the Rue des Ducs-de-Bar, which was the main thoroughfare in days gone by. It nods at the remains of some arcades that were once part of the ancient market but bypasses the elegant, triangular Place St-Pierre, overlooked by the Église St-Étienne. This is a fairly typical Gothic church dating from the fifteenth century but is widely known for a rather macabre sculpture by Ligier Richier called *Le Squelette*. It is something between a skeleton and a partly decomposed body representing René de Châlon, the Prince of Orange who was killed at the siege of St-Dizier in 1544, and stands in the mausoleum where his heart is said to be buried. A more conventional example of Richier's work is the crucifix in the Église Notre-Dame, a Romanesque church on the far side of the river that had to be restored after a fire in the seventeenth century. It is reached along the Rue du Bourg, lined with old houses presided over by gargoyles, as far as the Rue Maginot where the figure of a child with a bicycle is a memorial to Pierre and Ernest Michaux whose contribution to local transport is also enshrined in the Musée Barrois.

The road changes its name without altering direction, and crosses the river to reach a T-junction outside the Église Notre-Dame. From here the Rue Passage Supérieur heads for the Canal de la Marne au Rhin beyond which there is a right hand turn along the water's edge to the extensive grounds that surround the Château de Morbeaumont. Shortly afterwards it joins the N35 to Verdun, also known as the Voie Sacrée because it was the route once travelled by soldiers and prisoners between the town and the battlefields of World War I.

MEURTHE-ET-MOSELLE

Meurthe-et-Moselle is a very oddly shaped *département*. It consists of a fairly narrow strip down from the borders of Belgium and Luxembourg with Meuse on one side and Moselle on the other, coming to a bottleneck west of Metz. Thereafter it widens out considerably, crossing the Moselle river north of Pont-à-Mousson and extending eastwards for a brief meeting with Alsace near the Col du Donon. It is confined in the south by the Vosges with whom it shares a long, extremely convoluted border. The countryside in the far north is not particularly interesting but it becomes more attractive in the Parc Naturel Régional de Lorraine which the *département* shares with both Meuse and Moselle. The park is made up largely of marshland and relatively young forests and is home to wild boar, roebuck, otters and wild cats as well as all kinds of birds including booted eagles and green woodpeckers. Generally speaking Meurthe-et-Moselle is more agricultural than industrial and is liberally sprinkled with small villages, reached for the most part by a complicated network of minor roads and byways. It is also crossed by the GR5, the *Grande Randonnée* which links Holland with the Mediterranean. Its larger towns and places of especial interest are distributed fairly evenly throughout the whole area with the historic city of Nancy taking pride of place.

There is no doubt that **Nancy** has something to attract visitors of ❋ every persuasion, from ancient buildings and absorbing museums to centres of art, science and technology, not to mention botanical gardens, glass works and, above all, the incredible Place Stanislas. It is hardly surprising that the city's most atmospheric hotel, the Grand Hôtel de la Reine, ☎ 83 35 03 01, looks out over this remarkably exuberant square. The Altéa Thiers in the Rue Poincaré, ☎ 83 35 61 01, and the two Novotels on the outskirts are all larger and also have restaurants but none of them can claim to occupy anything half as historic as La Reine's one-time palace built in the eighteenth century. Several more modest hotels, almost invariably without restaurants, can be found within easy walking distance of the Place Stanislas and there are some excellent restaurants, although these have a tendency to close in January or August, or sometimes both, in addition to one day a week and possibly on public holidays as well.

Nancy does not claim to have any association with the Romans or the Gauls, who may well have had other, more convenient sites in mind. The city appears to have come into existence in the eleventh century when Gérard d'Alsace, who founded the hereditary dukedom of Lorraine, decided that he needed a castle-fortress to protect this part of his domain. It was burned down in 1228, rebuilt almost immediately and subsequently strengthened with encircling walls and towers which included the Porte de la Craffe. This rather formidable landmark on the street of the same name was used as a prison until shortly after the Revolution. It still has its dungeons whose walls are covered with graffiti left behind by a series of demoralised prisoners as well as a display of the instruments that were used to torture them. On a happier note there is also a collection of sculptures, most of them dating back to the late Middle Ages.

Quite close by, on the Grande-Rue, the Église et Couvent des Cordeliers has a great deal to recommend it. Part of the ancient monastery has been taken over by the Musée d'Arts et Traditions Populaires, full of everyday items connected with the life of the community. They include typical furniture, household goods and chattels and craftsmen's tools of every description, frequently incorporated into tableaux which makes them even more viewable. On the other hand the church is decidedly opulent as befits the last resting place of the dukes of Lorraine, nearly all of whom are buried in the crypt. Foremost among the artistic attractions are two contributions by local Renaissance artists, Mansuy Gauvain and Ligier Richier; namely the tomb of René II and the likeness of his second wife, Philippe de Gueldre, wearing the habit of the religious order to which she belonged when she died. Other things to look out for are a bas-relief of the Last Supper apparently inspired by Leonardo de Vinci, the seventeenth-century stalls and one or two paintings of the Virgin Mary. The Chapelle Ducale was added in 1607 on the orders of Duc Charles III just prior to his death in the following May. He was given a magnificent funeral that lasted intermittently for several weeks. His subjects maintained that no-one had ever seen anything like it, except, perhaps, for the coronation of an emperor at Frankfurt or of a king in the cathedral at Reims. Although it was an impossible event to follow adequately, the Chapelle Ducale has had its less spectacular moments much more recently. They included the lying-in-state of Maréchal Lyautey in 1934 and the marriage of Archduke Otto of Habsburg 17 years later.

The nearest place of interest to the Couvent des Cordeliers is the Palais Ducal, a few blocks away down the Grande-Rue on the opposite side. It started life in the thirteenth century but was already in a sorry state when René II set about rebuilding it after he had defeated Charles le Téméraire who fought hard to win the region for himself. However René's improvements were not nearly extrovert enough to suit Duc Antoine de Lorraine and before long the palace had a splendid new entrance, smothered in stone carvings, with Duc Antoine riding a mettlesome charger in a niche over the main door. The balconies and balustrades were given much the same treatment which makes it an ideal setting for the extremely well informed Musée Historique Lorraine.

Nothing appears to have escaped the notice of the curators. The Galerie d'Archéologie, in its own pavilion in the garden, is full of prehistoric discoveries, Celtic bits and pieces and Gallo-Roman remains. From here the history of Lorraine moves indoors, through the Middle Ages and up to the Galerie des Cerfs which concentrates on the dukes of Lorraine from the sixteenth to the eighteenth century. Everywhere there are pictures and tapestries, sculptures, miniatures and collections of china and earthenware. On the floor above the emphasis turns more towards politics, military matters and literature in the eighteenth and nineteenth centuries with a passing interest in popular religious art. Finally, the top floor is reserved for Lorraine during and after the restoration of the Third Republic and particularly to the part it played in wartime, especially throughout World War I.

The Palais du Gouvernement, on the nearby Place de Général de Gaulle, was once the residence of the governors of Lorraine and can be easily recognised by its colonnade, designed along Grecian lines and decorated with characters from mythology. The building faces down the Place de la Carrière, which could just as well be described as an avenue lined with elegant mansions and decorated with fountains, where riders used to exercise their horses in days gone by. At the far end is the Arc de Triomphe, built in the Roman style between 1754 and 1756 in honour of Louis XV whose likeness is flanked by various gods of war on one side and goddesses of peace on the other.

The king looks out directly on to the famous Place Stanislas, designed by Emmanuel Héré, whose massive wrought-iron gates

The incredible Place Stanislas in Nancy, is a masterpiece of design and stunningly beautiful

The Arc de Triomphe, built along Roman lines in honour of Louis XV, Nancy

partly obscured by gold, were the work of Jean Lamour. The square, which dazzles onlookers when the sun shines, takes its name from Stanislas Leszczynski, the deposed king of Poland whose daughter married Louis XV. The king promptly created his father-in-law Duc de Lorraine with the proviso that all his lands would revert to France eventually. The choice was a wise one. Stanislas proved to be an ideal governor in every respect and for the next 30 years his domain flourished, tolerance was practiced in every field including religion and he was able to indulge his passion for fine buildings. Undoubtedly his most eye-catching achievement was the complex which includes the Place Stanislas with its splendid fountains, black and gold iron tracery, hanging lamps adorned with crowns and a statue of Louis XV placed tactfully in the middle.

The Musée des Beaux-Arts occupies one of the surrounding mansions that were designed specially to complete the overall picture. It is crammed with paintings from the fourteenth century to the present day, the ground floor being reserved for comparatively modern French artists. Among the pictures on display are Manet's portrait of Méry Laurent and the *Bataille de Nancy* as visualised by Delacroix. Elsewhere there are works by Utrillo, Rubens, Tintoretto and members of the French school of the seventeenth and eighteenth centuries such as Boucher and Van Loo. Meanwhile the second floor is used almost exclusively for temporary exhibitions. The Hôtel de Ville, on the opposite side of the square from the Arc de Triomphe, also fits in admirably with its surroundings. Everything about it is in keeping, from the insignia of the House of Leszczynski to Jean Lamour's staircase, and the frescoes in the so-called Académie to the Grand Salon, opened by the Empress Eugénie in 1866.

The cathedral, which is not far from the Hôtel de Ville along the Rue Maurice Barrès and across the Rue St-Georges, dates from the early eighteenth century. It contains a number of chapels, some of whose grilles were created by Jean Lamour, and a fairly modest treasure consisting of a variety of small items, one or two of them about 1,000 years old. Other attractions scattered over several blocks in the vicinity include a fountain in the Place d'Alliance, commemorating the agreement reached between Louis XV and Marie Thérèse of Austria. There is also the decorative Maison des Adam on the Rue des Dominicains which belonged to two eighteenth-century sculptors, and the Église St-Sébastien in the Place Henri-Mengin that was restored in 1731 and has a typical Baroque façade.

Anyone who begins to find an undiluted diet of art and architecture a trifle indigestible can head for La Pépinière, a large attractive park with a rose garden, a sports stadium and a small zoo. For some reason the Musée de Zoologie is located in the Jardin Botanique on the opposite side of the Rue Ste-Catherine. The ground floor is given over to a tropical aquarium whose inhabitants come from far-flung corners of the world such as the Pacific Ocean, the Red Sea and the Amazon Basin, whereas the floor above contains zoological specimens.

The garden itself was created in 1758 and specialises mainly in Alpine plants. Its counterpart is a good deal further away, near the racecourse and the university at the far end of the Avenue du Général Leclerc. Known as the Jardin Botanique du Montet, it covers a large area and supports a sufficiently wide variety of trees and plants to keep enthusiastic gardeners occupied for hours. On the way to the Jardin Botanique du Montet, the Musée de l'École de Nancy is situated on the Rue Sergent-Blandan, near the military hospital. It was founded by Émile Gallé at the turn of the century and contains some striking examples of the work of his students and local craftsmen about 100 years ago. There are some beautiful pieces of glassware, inlaid furniture, leatherwork and pottery as well as examples of the sort of decorative art that was described as the 'Modern Style' in 1890 or thereabouts.

Almost as far from the Place Stanislas, but this time on the Avenue de Strasbourg, the Église Notre-Dame-de-Bon-Secours was built by Héré in 1738. It replaced a chapel that was constructed in the reign of René II to commemorate his victory over Charles le Téméraire and his Burgundian forces in 1477. Behind its Baroque façade the church contains a good deal that is well worth seeing. For example, there is the tomb of Stanislas le Manifique, the mausoleum of his wife Catherine Opalinska and a monument to Marie Leszczynska, the wife of Louis XV. Elsewhere are wrought-iron grilles by Jean Lamour, an impressive pulpit and choir stalls and an unusual statue of the Vierge de Miséricorde, shown protecting a number of small figures who have taken refuge under her cloak.

Further down the Avenue de Strasbourg, the Musée de l'Histoire du Fer contains more of interest than one might expect from a museum devoted entirely to iron. Its use is traced from prehistoric times and throughout the Middle Ages with highlights to demonstrate its role in the manufacture of weapons, as well as the part it played in artwork of various descriptions. One of the most popular exhibits is La Boyotte, an early steam engine that is in the section reserved for machinery. Meanwhile, anyone who prefers glass to iron can visit the historic Cristalleries Daum in the Rue des Cristalleries between the Canal de la Marne au Rhin and the River Meurthe, not all that far from La Pépinière. Here it is possible to watch the glassmakers at work and see a whole range of finished articles on display in the adjoining shop.

Visitors to Nancy who have interests other than sightseeing will also find plenty of ways to occupy their time. Apart from the racecourse there is a skating rink and facilities for tennis, swimming and riding as well as an 18-hole golf course quite close by. The Opéra Théâtre de Nancy in the Rue Ste-Catherine stages traditional performances with great aplomb while the Ballet Théâtre Français in the Rue Henri-Bazin has a repertoire ranging from Diaghilev to Miles Pendleton. Music of several different types plays a large part in the life of the city, encouraged by organisations like the Association pour la Musique Ancienne de Nancy and a well patronised school of rock music.

In addition to organised excursions there are any number of places to visit for motorists who prefer to explore on their own. One of the closest of these is the **Château de Fléville**, 9km (6 miles) to the south-east on the D71. It was originally designed as a fortress in the twelfth century but was completely altered some 400 years later and improved still further under the watchful eye of Duc Stanislas. It is built on three sides of a large court of honour, reached by a causeway across what was once a very businesslike moat. Nowadays grass has taken the place of water below the walls, guarded by a square keep at one corner and a round tower at the other. A guided tour of the château takes about half an hour and includes the chapel and various salons used by the dukes of Lorraine. Among them is the one chosen by Duc Stanislas for his bedroom. They are predictably elaborate, hung with pictures and filled with late eighteenth-century furniture.

Beyond the Château de Fléville, and not much more than 12km (7 miles) from the centre of Nancy along the N4, **St-Nicolas-de-Port** is known principally for its splendid basilica. The town has always been a commercial and industrial centre and was, incidentally, the place where Charles le Téméraire lost both the battle for Nancy and his life. It was shortly after this that work started on the present church, dedicated to St-Nicolas, the patron saint of Lorraine. It replaced an earlier sanctuary that was said to have been visited by Joan of Arc to ask for the saint's blessing on the battles that lay ahead. The church was completed in 1560 and, like its predecessor, is an important place of pilgrimage containing a relic of St-Nicolas. The façade has been compared very favourably with the cathedral at Toul, largely on account of its lofty towers and generally flamboyant style. The figure of the saint over the main door is attributed to Claude Richier, whose brother Ligier was one of Lorraine's most famous sculptors. The interior is equally impressive without being overwhelming although the 28m (92ft) pillars are said to be the tallest in France. The stained glass windows to the left of the choir, the Pietà and the fonts all date from the sixteenth century.

Down the road apiece, **Dombasle-sur-Meurthe** marks a point of contact between the River Meurthe and the Marne au Rhin Canal. It is a busy little place, much frequented by barges and other craft that are used to transport cargoes of iron and several different minerals. Its only obvious brush with the past is at nearby **Varangéville**, whose fifteenth-century church, built in the Gothic style, contains a veritable forest of pillars and a number of medieval sculptures.

Some 14km (9 miles) or so to the east of Dombasle-sur-Meurthe by road, but fractionally more along the river, **Lunéville** is a 'must' for anyone in search of elegant châteaux. It is a medium-sized town with nothing very exciting in the way of hotels although the Château d'Adomenil, 5km (3 miles) to the south, has an excellent restaurant and a handful of rooms for guests, ☎ 83 74 04 81. In the early eighteenth century Lunéville was the favourite playground of Duc Léopold de Lorraine, who greatly admired Louis XIV and was determined to copy the Sun King whenever possible. To this end he redesigned the existing château in the centre of the town in an effort to turn it into a miniature Versailles. Once the modifications were completed he entertained his court with music and dancing, theatrical performances, organised games and hunting. Stanislas was just as enamoured with this so-called 'Petit Versailles' and, after making a few more changes, spent a good deal of time there in the company of leading writers and artists of his day.

Much of the atmosphere still remains although the château is now a museum that concentrates almost entirely on local matters, such as the garrison that was stationed there in later years and a collection of the beautifully painted little china figures that are known as the Faïences de Lunéville. Adjoining the château are the large formal gardens of the Parc de Bosquets which were fully restored in 1946.

Opposite the château, between the Place de la 2nd Division-de-Cavalerie and the Rue République, the Musée de la Moto et du Vélo is small but extremely popular. It contains rather more than 200 models of three-wheel vehicles, mostly motor cycles and bicycles, built before 1939. Finally, a few blocks away, facing the Place St-Rémy, the Église St-Jacques is a delightful small church in the Baroque style. It was the brainchild of Germain Boffrand, who updated the château for Duc Léopold, and Emmanuel Héré, the architect responsible for the Place Stanislas in Nancy. A figure representing Time supports the clock over the main door with St Michel and St Jean Népomucène to the left and right of him respectively, while inside there is a fifteenth-century Pietà and some excellent wood carving.

Baccarat, 25km (15½ miles) from Lunéville down the N59, has very little in the way of tourist attractions apart from its Musée du Cristal, housed in an elderly mansion. The local glassworks have been turning out beautiful crystal since 1764 and the museum includes some exquisite examples that are more than 200 years old. Glassware of every sort is on display, some of it contemporary, ranging from brightly coloured to clear, paper-thin exhibits as well as intricately engraved pieces and examples of the original glassblowers art. Naturally glass is used to good effect in the Église St-Rémy, built in 1957. Its pièce de résistance is *La Creation du Monde*, a large work consisting of glass in literally dozens of different colours and held in place with concrete. The visit makes a pleasant day out from Nancy which is only 60km (37 miles) away.

The only place of any interest to tourists in the far north of Meurthe-et-Moselle is **Longwy**, and even then it is hardly worth making a special trip unless you happen to be passing that way. It was the site of a Roman camp long before the town was passed from hand to hand by the Ducs de Luxembourg, the Comtes de Bar and the Ducs de Lorraine, ending up as part of France in the seventeenth century. Despite the fact that Longwy was fortified by Vaubin during the reign of Louis XIV it was occupied on three different occasions before 1871 and again by the Germans in two World Wars. The whole place is highly industrial and nothing of moment has been preserved from the early days with the exception of an extremely modest Roman church near Mont-St-Martin. However, the nearby village of **Cons-la-Grandville** on the D172 boasts a large Renaissance château which is open to visitors while, beyond it, the Fort de Fermont is a grim reminder of the ill-fated Maginot Line.

To the north of Nancy, and about half way along the main road to Metz, **Pont-à-Mousson** is a different matter altogether. For example, there is the Place Duroc with its arcaded mansions that have been presenting a more or less united front for the past 400 years. Among the most outstanding of these are the Maison des Sept Péchés Capitaux, suitably decorated, and the Château d'Amour that once played host to the dukes of Lorraine. A comparative newcomer is the eighteenth-century Hôtel de Ville which has a nice line in tapestries on the first floor.

Several of the nearby streets have their own Renaissance mansions, especially the Rue Clemenceau and the Rue St-Laurent which takes its name from the adjoining church at the back of the Hôtel de Ville. Although the Église St-Laurent is somewhat older than its

neighbours only the chancel and the transept are original, the remainder having been added bit by bit until the façade was completed
in 1895. In some respects it is not unlike the Église St-Martin on the
far side of the Moselle river, close to the Ancien Collège des Jésuites.
This was originally home to an important university in the Middle
Ages, but it suffered considerably during the Thirty Years War and
was eventually transferred to Nancy.

A block or so down river is the massive Abbaye des Prémontrés
which was in turn a monastery, a seminary and a hospital before
being taken over by the Centre Culturel de Rencontre in 1964. A fair
amount of time is needed to look over the earlier part of the building
which includes the church, a large cloister and the upper floors,
reached by three different but quite impressive staircases. These
days the abbey is frequently used for exhibitions and it is also the
headquarters of the Centre Européen d'Art Sacré. Both the town and
the Butte de Mousson on the outskirts were very much in the line of
fire when the American army under General Patton engaged the
German forces there in September 1944. There are some ruins of a
feudal château that belonged to the Comtes de Bar and anyone with
sufficient energy to climb to the summit of the Butte de Mousson will
find a small modern chapel and a most rewarding view.

The Forêt de Haye, to the west of Nancy, is not really one of the
large recognised parks. It is more of a wide open space with few
roads apart from the *autoroute* and the N4, which keep each other
company right through the middle, and only a very occasional
hamlet. It is bordered in the north by the Moselle which makes a wide
sweep round the elderly village of **Liverdun** on its way to Toul.
Anyone in search of peace and quiet, an attractive site, good food and
a pleasant game of golf need look no further than Liverdun. Des
Vannes, in the Rue Porte-Haute, is a first class restaurant with a
handful of rooms attached, while its *résidence* provides both a garden
and some additional rooms, ☎ 83 24 46 01. For sightseers the main
attractions are the sixteenth-century gate at the entrance to the
village, arcades of comparable vintage in the Place de la Fontaine and
a much older church that was consecrated in 1261.

On the other hand, motorists who choose the main road to Toul
can stop off at the **Parc de la Forêt de Haye**, just 9km (6 miles) from
Nancy. This is essentially a leisure park with sports facilities, picnic
sites, marked paths, a little zoo and two contrasting museums. They
are the Musée de l'Aéronautique whose interests are confined to the
beginning of the twentieth century and the Musée de l'Auto with
dozens of cars including one that belonged to Georges Pompidou.

The old quarter of **Toul**, 23km (14 miles) from Nancy by the shortest route, is a good example of a fortified medieval town. There are several ways in and out through the defending walls, such as the Porte Jeanne d'Arc, the Porte de France and the Porte de Metz which owes its existence to Vaubin. The streets tend to swerve rather than twist and turn and many of them converge on the Église St-Gengoult and the nearby Place des Trois Évêchés. The church was built between the thirteenth and the fifteenth centuries and is justifiably proud of its ancient stained glass windows depicting scenes from the lives of Christ, St Nicolas and St Gengoult. The cloister was added afterwards and is remarkably elegant with its decorative columns, pointed arches and intricate stone carving.

The Rue du Général-Gengoult, quite close by, has rather more than its fair share of viewable old houses, at least one of which, number 8, has been there for about 600 years. The street makes a right-hand turn eventually to join the Rue Porte des Cordeliers about two blocks away from the Hôtel de Ville. This was previously the palace of the bishops and stands at right angles to the former Cathédrale St-Étienne whose gloriously flamboyant façade overlooks the Place Charles de Gaulle. The interior is pleasantly uncluttered, with a high nave, stained glass windows and the grave of St Gérard, who was Bishop of Toul in the eleventh century. It is situated to the left of the chancel while on the right, next to a small Renaissance chapel, there are steps leading to the cloister. This has stood the test of time extremely well and includes among its decorative carvings a rather nice collection of gargoyles.

Toul is not a very good place to look for somewhere to stay but as it is so close to Nancy this should not present any problems. Nor, for that matter, are there any really comfortable hotels in the south of the *département*, although there are one or two places that could usefully be included in a day's outing from the city.

Vézelise, for example, is on the D904 from Toul and also within a few kilometres of the main road from Nancy to Mirecourt, in the Vosges. This ancient capital of the Comtes de Vaudémont still has its covered markets, a Hôtel de Ville dating from 1561 and a medieval church complete with its original stained glass windows. On the opposite side of the D913, and reached by way of the D9 through Tantonville, the **Château d'Haroué** has plenty to offer its casual visitors. Most of the existing building was designed by Germain Boffrand, the architect who was responsible for the château at Lunéville. Built on much earlier foundations, it has a moat, a typical court of honour with wrought-iron work provided by Jean Lamour and statues in the grounds attributed to Guibal, who was also involved in beautifying the Place Stanislas in Nancy. A guided tour of the château takes in the chapel and the apartments of the princes of Beauvau-Craon, furnished with items that once belonged to Louis XVIII and hung with pictures and tapestries.

Due south of Vézelise, **Sion** has been attracting large numbers of pilgrims for several hundred years. In addition to the little eight-eenth-century church with its much older statue of Notre-Dame-de-Sion and plaques recalling some of the major pilgrimages, there is a

The Ancienne Cathédrale St-Étienne at Toul

very modest hotel and an equally self-effacing archaeological mu-seum. This traces the history of the so-called Colline Inspirée, the area between Sion and Vaudémont which was regarded as sacred by the Celts some 2,000 years ago. Their pagan gods were soon replaced by Christianity and later St-Gérard, as Bishop of Toul, officially declared it to be a holy place. The banner of Notre-Dame-de-Sion was carried into battle by Renée II when he defeated the

Burgundians who were attacking Nancy. More recently vast crowds of pilgrims have gathered here after each major war to give thanks to the Virgin for the return of peace. There is a memorable view from the top of the Mont de la Paix but as yet no road leading up to the summit.

A very minor scenic road, described variously as the D53 or the Corniche Gaston Canel, runs south from Sion, past the hilltop monument to Maurice Barrès and then round to **Vaudémont** where there are the remains of a ruined château. From here any number of little country roads set off in all directions, keeping a great many small rural communities in touch with one another. For motorists with enough time in hand they provide a choice of routes to either the D904 or the D913 which is the easiest and most direct way back to Nancy.

MOSELLE

Moselle accounts for a good quarter of the province of Lorraine, sharing its northern and north-eastern borders with Luxembourg and Germany, with whom it has a certain amount in common. Although it is liberally sprinkled with towns and villages, a great many of these are mainly concerned with various types of industry and, consequently, areas like the Pays du Fer, in the north-west, and the Carling-Merlebach region to the east, have little to offer the average visitor. Even the countryside in places is fairly nondescript but nevertheless there are plenty of things to see as long as one is prepared to look for them.

For anyone driving in from the west, especially along the A4 *autoroute*, the best place to stop is obviously **Metz**. The city has been ❊ an important centre for nearly 2,000 years, favoured by the Romans and later by the Franks under Charlemagne. At one time it was the capital of the kingdom of Austrasia, but became a free commune governed by its wealthy residents during the Middle Ages before being annexed by France in 1559.

Because of its strategic position on the Moselle river Metz has suffered a number of quite spectacular sieges. When the Franco-Prussian War broke out in 1870 François Bazaine, the commander of the Third Army Corps, withdrew to Metz following his defeat at Gravelotte. However, after about 2 months he surrendered with his entire force of 173,000 men and handed over vast quantities of equipment to the Prussians, who then had to protect him from the fury of the local inhabitants. After the war he was tried by a court-martial and sentenced to death but he managed to escape to Spain where he died in 1888. Meanwhile, Metz had become part of Germany under the Treaty of Frankfurt in 1871 and was only returned to France at the end of World War I. The last battle for Metz took place in 1944 when a section of the American army under General Walker captured the city from the retreating Germans, but only after an attack that had lasted for more than 2 months.

These days Metz is once again very commercially minded, but at the same time it pays considerable attention to other matters such as religion and education. It has about fifty different churches, a university founded in 1972 and a European Institute of Ecology. Nor is the city short of hotels, ranging from the up-market Sofitel in the Place Paraiges, ☎ 87 74 57 27 and the Altéa St-Thiébault in the Place St-Thiébault, ☎ 87 36 17 69 to smaller, less expensive establishments, most of which only provide their guests with a continental breakfast. However there are plenty of restaurants to be found in the vicinity and just as many on the outskirts, such as the Belle-Vue on the Rue Pange, near the Palais des Congrès, on the way to St-Avold.

One of the first places to visit in Metz is undoubtedly the Cathédrale St-Étienne which started life as the adjoining churches of Notre-Dame-la-Ronde and St-Étienne in the twelfth century, but was up-dated out of all recognition some 200 years later. It is an impressive building with towers and pinnacles and some interesting stone carving round the doors. The Portail de Notre-Dame-la-Ronde is decorated with strange animals and scenes from the lives of two saints in addition to King David, while the Portail Louis XV is watched over by statues of various prophets including Daniel. It is said that he was originally designed in the early 1900s to look like the German Emperor William II, but 40 years later his whiskers were removed to make the resemblance less obvious.

Inside, apart from the high, comparatively narrow nave, its most outstanding features are the stained-glass windows. Sadly, the fourteenth-century rose window over the main door was altered when the Grand Portail was reconstructed in 1766, but there are several other beautiful examples from the Middle Ages, as well as some modern windows that are the work of Jacques Villon and Marc Chagall. The first section of the nave was part of the old church of Notre-Dame-la-Ronde, while the transept dates from the end of the fifteenth century with steps leading down to a much older crypt. The cathedral treasure, or what was left of it after the Revolution, is housed in the Grande Sacristie on the opposite side. It contains, among other relics, a gold ring that belonged to St-Arnoult, the crimson silk Chape de Charlemagne enriched with golden eagles, an enamelled reliquary and a variety of religious artifacts.

From the Place d'Armes, beside the cathedral, the Rue Chanoine-Collin leads directly to the Musée d'Art et d'Histoire, housed in the fifteenth-century Couvent des Petits Carmes. Constructed on the site of a much older building it has the remains of some Gallo-Roman baths down in the basement, embellished with pagan gods such as Mithras and Jupiter. Elsewhere there are plenty of examples of medieval art, a splendid Baroque staircase and some Renaissance murals that were only uncovered in 1982. Other exhibits include paintings, some of them contemporary, a military section that concentrates on weapons, uniforms and accessories from the time of Napoléon Bonaparte onwards and another dealing exclusively with natural history.

Most other places of interest are quite widely distributed over the older part of the city which lies between two probing fingers of the Moselle river. This involves a good deal of walking because the majority of the streets are restricted to one-way traffic and without a good map and a competent map reader it is possible to drive round and round without actually getting anywhere. However, by sticking to the encircling boulevards, motorists can easily find their way to the impressive Porte des Allemands, crossing the water between the Boulavard Paixhans and the Rue André Maginot, within striking distance of the N3. This splendid medieval complex consists of a typically uncompromising fortified gateway, complete with battlements and two formidable towers, on the far bank and an older, more 'Grimm's Fairytale' type of fortress giving the town a second line of defence on the other. The latter consists of matching round towers with slate-covered roofs closely resembling witches' hats that make them look like a couple of gigantic pepperpots, with a smaller Tour aux Sorcières in attendance. The two gateways are linked by a bridge, built over a single arch and edged with elderly arcades.

On the opposite side of the main thoroughfare the Église St-Eucaire, on the Rue des Allemands, has a twelfth-century tower, a thirteenth-century façade and several adaptations carried out over the next 200 years. The result is a trifle odd but nonetheless fascinating. From here it is only a few blocks to the Église St-Maximin, on the Rue Mazelle, which also started life in the twelfth century and is known mainly for its stained-glass windows. Roughly the same distance away, the Place St-Louis with its arcaded medieval mansions was once the centre of the town, both literally and commercially because it was here that the merchants gathered to change their money. Nearby are two more small churches, the Église St-Martin with obvious Roman connections and the Église Notre-Dame-de-l'Assumption that is more closely allied to Louis XV with confessionals that would have appealed to Madame Pompadour.

It is hardly surprising that Metz has so many churches when you realise that it has three saints all to itself. The earliest was St-Clément, the first Bishop of Metz, who is said to have fought and defeated paganism in the form of a terrible monster with poisonous breath at some time during the third century. The next was St-Livier who, after having been decapitated by Attila the Hun, calmly picked up his head and went off into the mountains with it to dig his own grave. St-Arnoult's claim to sainthood was much more factual. He was an important local dignitary, married with two children, when the seventh-century townspeople implored him to become Bishop of Metz. He agreed, and to simplify matters his wife went into a convent, but in her case virtue was considered to be its own, if only, reward.

While on the subject of small churches, two others that are just as well worth seeing are tucked away between the Boulevard Poincaré and the Avenue Ney on the opposite side of the old town from the Porte des Allemands. They are the octagonal Chapelle des Templiers, dating from the early thirteenth century, and the Église St-Pierre-aux-Nonnains, said to be the oldest church in France. It was originally part of a Benedictine monastery founded some 1,400 years ago but abolished in the sixteenth century and incorporated into a

The Porte des Allemands dates from the thirteenth century, Metz

citadel which has also disappeared. The church still has traces of its Roman origins as well as some excavations next door which may or may not be the remains of the public baths.

This is probably the most restful area in Metz with its Esplanade overlooked by the eighteenth-century Palais de Justice, the nearby Lac des Cygnes, half-hidden in the park, and views across the river towards the university. Slightly downstream, beyond the Pont Moyen, the river divides to form an island, more or less level with the cathedral, which is the site of both the national theatre and the prefecture.

In addition to everything else the city prides itself on being an important drama and music centre, taking an informed interest in everything from opera and ancient music to jazz and the development of what it calls *musique contemporaine*. Visitors are encouraged to visit the Centre Européen d'Écologie in the ancient Couvent des Récollets, admire the massive neo-Roman railway station built by the Germans in 1908, go shopping, swim or play golf at the 9-hole course 14km (9 miles) away to the south on the D913.

As far as excursions are concerned, anyone with a young family to entertain would probably head for **Walibi-Schtroumpf**, an amusement park near Semecourt on the N52, fractionally south of the A4. In some ways it is reminiscent of Disney World with a whole host of attractions including an enormous switchback, slides of every description and a small train made up entirely of cars instead of an engine pulling carriages. There is a swimming pool filled with multi-coloured balls in place of water where children can play quite safely, trips round the lake by boat, restaurants and cafeterias and, of course, resident wallabies who look rather like bright blue gnomes in nightcaps. It is open all day from late April to early September including Sundays and holidays.

There is practically nothing of interest to see in the area west of Metz, apart from mines and industrial installations, with the possible exception of **Gravelotte**, on the N3. The village played a minor role during the Franco-Prussian War and has a reasonably informative military museum with exhibits obtained from both the opposing armies. **Gorze**, slightly to the south, is somewhat larger and can trace its history back to the eighth century when it was founded by Chrodegang, one of the saintly bishops of Metz. It has a small church with a figure of Christ attributed to Ligier Richier, the remains of its ecclesiastical palace and quite an impressive Roman aqueduct built in the first century AD about 8km (5 miles) away to the east.

The countryside to the south-east of Metz has rather more to recommend it. **Marsal**, for example, just off the D38 on the edge of the

Parc Régional de Lorraine, has some Gallo-Roman remains and the Collegiate Church of St-Léger which was started in AD441 but did not achieve its full potential until the twelfth century. The village has always been involved in the production of salt and was considered to be of sufficient importance for Vauban to take a hand in its fortifications, although only the much-restored Porte de France has survived. Just below the gateway is the Maison du Sel which traces the history of the industry and the part it played in the overall economy of the country. **Vic-sur-Seille**, further to the west on the D38, also grew rich as a result of its salt deposits and has an elderly Couvent des Carmes and the small medieval church of St-Martin as well as a fifteenth-century mint.

Sarrebourg, still further to the east, can be reached quite easily by way of the D955 and the N4. In its infancy Sarrebourg belonged to the Romans. Later it became the property of the bishops of Metz, passed into the hands of the dukes of Lorraine and eventually took its place as a very minor jewel in the crown of Louis XIV. Its thirteenth-century Chapelle des Cordeliers is remarkable for its gigantic stained-glass window, created out of 13,000 different pieces by Marc Chagall. Not far away, in the Avenue de France, the Musée du Pays de Sarrebourg dabbles mainly in archaeological discoveries dating back to Roman times, augmented by a collection of fourteenth-century ceramics. Somewhat further away, on the Rue de Verdun, there is a cemetery containing the graves of many thousands of prisoners who died during World War I. The town also has a perfectly adequate hotel, the France in the Avenue de France, ☎ 87 03 21 47 for anyone who wants a bed while waiting to explore the surrounding area.

The different places that can be visited within less than 20km (12 miles) are surprisingly varied. For example, 10km (6 miles) due south along the D44 through Hess, where there is a small, partly Roman church, and then via the D96, **Hartzviller** is known for its glass factory whose craftsmen turn out articles of all descriptions. From here it is possible to explore some of the twisting byways or follow the road round to join the D45. This links Sarrebourg with **Dabo**, a popular tourist centre that boasts a small *auberge* and the adjacent Rocher de Dabo surmounted by the chapel of St Leon. This little church marks the highest point in the *département* and consequently has a splendid view. Alternatively, anyone who is interested in Roman remains can visit the excavations at **St-Ulrich**, 4km (2 miles) to the north-east near Haut-Clocher. A good deal has been uncovered since 1894 and there is a tiny museum on the site full of bits and pieces that were left lying about in what must have been an important settlement.

On the other hand, motorists in search of more recent history can take the N4 to **Phalsbourg** which supplied Napoléon with so many outstanding officers that he christened it 'the breeding ground of the brave'. Apart from the main gates — the decorative Porte de France and the Porte d'Allemagne with its plaque commemorating Goethe's visit in 1770 — there is a small museum in the Hôtel de Ville. It recalls the three sieges of Phalsbourg (in 1814, 1815 and 1870) as well as its liberation in 1944, along with traditional costumes, uniforms, weapons and various works by local artists. From here the quickest way back to Metz is along the *autoroute* but anyone with time in hand might enjoy deviating to **Fenetrange**, a medieval town in the so-called 'pond country' which covers a large section of the Parc Regional de Lorraine.

Further to the north, but still to the east of Metz, there is a clutch of small places which, although not among the *département's* leading tourist attractions, are nevertheless quite interesting. **Sarreguemines**, for instance, has been making pottery and china for centuries and has preserved a representative selection in a minute museum which occupies part of an old mansion in the Rue Poincaré. **Zetting**, marginally to the south-east, has an attractive little church with an antiquated tower and a 600-year-old *mise au tombeau*. Meanwhile **Bitche**, some 35km (22 miles) along the N62 and somewhat out on a limb, weighs in with a citadel built in 1741 on the site of an earlier fortress designed by Vauban. It successfully resisted the attacks launched against it during the Franco-Prussian War, which is more than can be said for the Fort du Simershof in 1940. Located 4km (2 miles) to the west on the D35, it was completed in 1935 as part of the Maginot Line with all the necessary tunnels, living quarters, storerooms and military paraphernalia, as well as a little train, but it was outflanked and fell to the German army without ever having really justified its existence.

Thionville, only 29km (18 miles) north of Metz on the A31 *autoroute*, is the second largest town in the *département*. It grew up round a Merovingian fortress and was known to the Franks as *Theodonis Villa* at a time when it was one of Charlemagne's favourite residences. In the thirteenth century it was enlarged and strengthened by the Counts of Luxembourg, after which it had a somewhat chequered career. It belonged in turn to the Burgundians, the Habsburgs and even the Spanish before being handed over to France under the Treaty of the Pyrénées in 1659. The town's ancient defences were down-graded by the Germans between 1870 and 1914, after which the inhabitants of Thionville decided that they would rather ignore any further conflicts and turn their attention to commerce and industry instead.

The sixteenth-century paved Place d'Armes in the attractive town of Phalsbourg

One result of all these upheavals is that there are only one or two places of interest in Thionville, in addition to a handful of modest hotels and a restaurant with a few rooms in the Place Luxembourg. The oldest reminder of the past is the Tour aux Puces, overlooking the Moselle river and the Quai Marchal. It is all that is left of the original fortress and gets its name from an ancient legend. Apparently a certain princess, who was waiting there for Charlemagne to return from one of his campaigns, came to an untimely end when she was eaten alive by fleas. However, this has not prevented the authorities from using it for the Musée d'Archéologie et d'Histoire where one can wander round inspecting its not very inspiring exhibits with no fear of getting bitten.

 The Château de la Grange on the outskirts, within a stone's throw of the N53, is infinitely more attractive for several reasons, none of which have anything to do with fleas. It was built in 1731 by Robert de Cotte on the remains of part of the old citadel which were acquired by the Marquis de Fouquet in 1652. It is both elegant and very well maintained, hung with paintings and early seventeenth-century Flemish tapestries. A guided tour of the château includes the large kitchen, the dining room with its lofty, extremely decorative porcelain stove that was made specially for the marquis and a bathroom with a bathtub fashioned out of a single block of white marble, that once belonged to Pauline Bonaparte. In addition there are reception rooms distinguished by their different colours, an ancient Persian tapestry, a collection of beautiful Oriental china and some excellent furniture.

Within striking distance of the château, the Fort de Guentrange was built by the Germans in 1899 but was taken over intact by the French army at the end of World War I. Several years later it was incorporated into the Maginot Line which stretched from La Ferté in Champagne on the Belgian border, to Fort à Chaux, well to the north of Strasbourg, and then down the Rhine to Switzerland. It was an ambitious idea in abstract that simply did not work in practice and like the other main defensive strongpoints the Fort de Guentrange proved to be less than useless. Its only attraction these days is a stairway up to a viewing platform which commands a useful view over Thionville and the valley of the Moselle.

VOSGES

There are quite a few different places to choose as a base for anyone who intends to spend some time in the Vosges. It is a *département* with an enormous variety of attractions, everything from sailing to skiing and ancient castles to a thriving casino or two, as well as scenic drives through the mountains, craft workshops and imaginative museums. The largest town is **Épinal**, more or less in the centre, with a scattering of fairly ordinary hotels, some excellent restaurants and a motel on the N57 at Golbey, just on the outskirts.

Architecturally the town has comparatively little to recommend it apart from the remains of an ancient château and the Basilique St-Maurice, parts of which date from the eleventh century. Its most famous asset is the Musée des Vosges et de l'Imagerie, standing at one end of a large island in the middle of the Moselle river. Some 200 years ago a local factory began to perfect the art of colour printing, turning out a host of stylised figures in primary colours, usually of historical or storybook characters, that soon became known as the Images d'Epinal. A selection of these distinctive engravings, mounted on wood, have been set up along the roadside in the vicinity of the town but they are only a foretaste of the variety on display in the Musée International de l'Imagerie on the first floor of the building. In addition to the local collection there are examples from other leading centres such as Chartres, Metz, Rouen and Avignon.

Elsewhere in the Musée des Vosges are drawings and paintings by famous masters like Rembrandt, Brueghel and Van Loo as well as by more modern artists including Picasso. Also on display are all the various bits and pieces so dear to the hearts of archaeologists, among them old coins and medals, fragments of ancient architecture, statues and a battered tombstone from the time of the Romans. One section has been allocated to more everyday matters in the life of the community, described as the Exposition Ethnographique et Folklorique. Just inside the entrance to the museum is a counter covered with books and other paraphernalia for sale, mostly concerned with the Images d'Épinal. Some of the items are quite expensive but they do make excellent presents and unusual souvenirs.

The Basilique St-Maurice, in the centre of the old town bordering on the river, is a mixture of different styles accumulated for the most part between the eleventh and fifteenth centuries, although it suffered a certain amount of damage during the Revolution. The interior is quite impressive without containing anything of outstanding merit. The Église Notre-Dame, a considerable walk away over two bridges and along the Avenue Mar de Lattre, was rebuilt in the 1950s and is therefore predictably modern in every respect. The Parc du Château, which takes its name from a smattering of ancient ruins, is separated from the old quarter by the Rue Abbé-Friesenhauser and the Rue d'Ambrail. It is pleasantly wooded and is essentially a leisure park with a small lake, sports facilities and a mini-zoo. The only other attractions are the large Parc du Cours beside the river, complete with a rose garden, and the Imagerie Pellerin gallery, out on a limb a bit further downstream off the Quai de Dogneville. This was founded in 1796 to keep alive the expertise that created the Images d'Épinal and is extremely interesting and well informed.

To the south of Épinal, about 7km (4 miles) along the N57 near Dinozé, there is a vast American cemetery with a chapel and a memorial to more than 7,000 men who died in action towards the end of World War II.

From this point the N57 follows the contours of the river down to **Remiremont**, which has nothing very prepossessing in the way of hotels but makes up for this with some quite attractive houses and a picturesque main street lined with arcades whose pillars are swathed in flowers. Remiremont was once the site of a famous nunnery that flourished under a long line of regal abbesses until the Revolution put an end to all that. Its Gothic church of Notre-Dame was given a new façade and bell-tower about 200 years ago, when the adjacent Palais Abbatial was also updated. The church was supplied with an ornate altar-piece but few if any changes were made to the eleventh-century crypt. Most of the items preserved from the abbey can be seen in one or other of the town's Municipal Museums. The

Musée Municipal in the Rue Charles de Gaulle has a section devoted to old manuscripts and tapestries while, at the same time, taking an interest in sculpture, painting and ornithology. Meanwhile its counterpart in the Rue Genéral-Humbert has its fair share of documents, statues and objects d'art, traces the history of the region and backs on to part of the original abbey gardens embellished with ornamental fountains and a few scattered remnants from the past.

Although Épinal can supply its visitors with boating, riding and a flying club, those in search of an up-market hotel would be well advised to press on to either **Plombières-les-Bains** or Gérardmer, depending on the type of holiday they have in mind. The former, as its name implies, is a popular spa and is only 30km (19 miles) away on the D434 to Xertigny and thereafter along the D63. The site was originally discovered by the Romans who seldom missed a natural health-giving spring. They made good use of it until their large thermal centre was overrun by the next wave of invaders who were apparently less obsessed with cleanliness. However, things took a turn for the better during the Middle Ages under the patronage of the Ducs de Lorraine. In due course the spa provided a cure for Montaigne, played host to Voltaire, and entertained Louis XV's daughters, Adélaïde and Victoire, on more than one occasion. The Empress Joséphine and Queen Hortense also found it very much to their liking but Napoléon III insisted on making a number of improvements before he met Cavour there to discuss matters of state and a possible union between France and Italy.

There are several different baths dotted about, almost within sight of each other, busily treating patients for digestive troubles or rheumatism. The Bain Romain, for example, is distinguished by some venerable masonry and a statue of Augustus. Bonaparte watches over the Bain National, which was rebuilt in 1935 behind its original façade, while Napoléon III presides over his own addition on the Avenue des Etats-Unis, conveniently close to the Grand Hôtel, ☎ 29 66 00 03 and the casino. The Musée Louis-Français is more of a picture gallery than a museum with works by the painter concerned and several of his friends. The town is equipped with a variety of fairly modest hotels and apartments in addition to the occasional camping site and encourages its guests to explore the surrounding area. Among the outlying attractions are the Fontaine Stanislas, a bare 3km (2 miles) to the south-west and, beyond it, the Musée Hippomobile in Aillevillers-et-Lyaumont with its collection of horsedrawn vehicles from the nineteenth century. Anyone in search of souvenirs might well prefer to spend some time in **La Rochère** where the glass factory, founded in 1475, produces some most attractive pieces. It is possible to watch the glassmakers and engravers at work during the season, except in August when they are all on holiday and only the shop and the museum are open.

Gérardmer, 41km (25 miles) from Épinal beyond Remiremont, is generally considered to be the holiday playground of the Vosges. It is a pleasant, rapidly expanding and quite modern town built at one end of a sizeable lake high up in the mountains and is equally popular in both summer and winter. There are no architectural treasures or museums but its Office de Tourisme claims to be the oldest in France. The whole place is sports orientated. There are plenty of opportunities for sailing and boating as well as pedalos for hire. Waterskiing and windsurfing are positively encouraged while, for less energetic visitors, it lays on trips by launch around the lake and organises excursions into the surrounding countryside to admire waterfalls, valleys created by ancient glaciers and vantage points commanding some memorable views. The town has two covered swimming pools, a skating rink and tennis courts in addition to facilities for riding, fishing and playing bowls. Its winter attractions, which naturally include the casino, are augmented by nine or ten ski lifts, a school for cross-country skiing and equipment for hire.

There are plenty of hotels in and around Gérardmer, some of them purpose built for winter sports. At the top of the list is the Grand Hôtel Bragard in the Place Tilleul, ☎ 29 63 06 31 closely followed by the Réserve on the Esplanade du Lac, ☎ 39 63 21 60 and the Hostellerie Bas-Rupts et Chalet Fleuri, ☎ 29 63 09 25, 4km (2 miles) away on the D486 towards La Bresse. This is, in fact, an excellent restaurant with a few rooms for guests. However, there is an even better reason for driving out to **L-diere**, on the D23 north-east of Xonrupt-Longemer. It is a chalet-type relais surrounded by woods with a four-in-one museum which it insists is the most important private collection of its kind in Europe. For gardeners it has greenhouses full of cacti, some of them as much as 7m (23ft) tall. Then there are butterflies and insects from many different parts of the world such as the Morphos Cypris from Columbia whose wings change colour, the giant Australian Hercules and Leaf-Butterflies from Madagascar, to mention but a few. The third facet of the museum is made up of primitive masks and wood carvings, some lifelike and quite unusual while others are large and predictable. Finally there is a collection of fossils, ores and minerals that are very viewable in themselves but especially so when they are subjected to ultra-violet light. This party-piece is called 'The Light in the Darkness' and produces some fascinating changes that keep the subsequent discussions going for hours.

The whole area to the south and east of Gérardmer is mountainous, pitted with lakes, adorned with forests and etched with paths and cart tracks, many of which it would be unwise to attempt in the average family car. On the other hand there are a number of very serviceable routes twisting and turning from one valley to another. From Xonrupt-Longemer the D417 skirts the lake, passes the Roche du Diable, that can really only be appreciated on foot, and joins the Route des Crêtes in Alsace at the Col de la Schlucht.

The D8, to the north, heads for **St-Dié**, a relatively modern town on the River Meurthe which has been burned down on at least four different occasions, most recently in 1944 when the retreating German army set fire to it. Nevertheless it still has a nucleus of old buildings, all huddled together round the cathedral. In its infancy St-Dié consisted of little more than a few cottages in the shadow of a Benedictine monastery founded by St-Déodat in the seventh century. This has completely disappeared and in its place there is the combined Cathédrale St-Dié and the Église Notre-Dame de Galilée, joined by a Gothic cloister. They are both typically medieval although the façade of the cathedral was considerably updated about 200 years ago.

The Lake at Gérardmer is ideal for energetic pursuits or relaxation

The ancient episcopal palace has been replaced by the Musée Municipal whose interests are many and varied, ranging from archaeology to a splendid collection of more than 300 birds that make their homes in the Vosges. Just as much attention is paid to the achievements of Jules Ferry, the French statesman who was born in St-Dié in 1832 and was twice Premier of France before he was murdered by a fanatic in 1893. Among the items on display are documents, photographs, pictures and other memorabilia that belonged to him and various members of his family. The adjoining Bibliotheque is filled with books and manuscripts concerned largely with local history.

St-Dié is only 30km (19 miles) from Gérardmer and has some small but quite acceptable hotels which come in handy for anyone who wants to explore the area in greater depth. Much of the surrounding countryside was inhabited long before the Benedictine monks founded their monastery there in the seventh century. Evidence of this can be seen at the partly excavated Camp Celtique de la Bure. However this entails a long walk through the woods after turning off the N59 to the right through Le Pêcherie. Archaeologists have discovered traces of human habitation from about 3,000BC, overlaid with fractionally younger defensive ditches and marks that look suspiciously like cart tracks. It seems as though the residents took flight for some reason or other, or were driven out by either the Romans or the Gauls. Either way, the settlement was left to moulder without interruption for another 1,600 years.

St-Dié was by no means the only religious centre founded at about the same time in this part of the Vosges. In fact, there are two quite obvious reminders on the way to Senones. At the village of **Étival-Clairefontaine**, some 12km (7 miles) away, just off the N59, the local church has preserved part of a stairway that once connected the transept with the ancient monastery of Prémontrés. Papermaking has kept the villagers occupied for about 400 years but the factory has now outgrown its original premises — a waterside mill dating from 1512. A few kilometres beyond the turning off to Étival-Clairefontaine, on the opposite side of the N59, the D424 heads eastwards towards Senones. On the way it passes through **Moyenmoutier** which had its own abbey in the seventh century but contents itself these days with a large church that was completely rebuilt some 200 years ago.

Senones is a nice little town which also owes its existence to an ancient Benedictine abbey. At one time it was the capital of the principality of Salm but in 1793 the townspeople demanded to be reunited with France. They got their way and now look back nostalgically to the good old days with special celebrations every year in July and August. The Maison Abbatiale is open to visitors daily except on Sundays, with special emphasis on the *appartement* occupied by Dom Calmet, one of the last of the abbots. He was an extremely learned man who attracted the attention of Voltaire, and there are reminders of him, several other abbots and the Princes of Salm on display in the various showcases. When Dom Calmet died the sculptor Falguière was chosen to design his tomb in the church nearby. An added attraction for railway enthusiasts is the little steam train that operates between Senones and Étival, a distance of about 10km (6 miles), mainly for the benefit of tourists.

Situated in the opposite direction from Gérardmer, and separated by 14km (9 miles) of typical mountain road, **La Bresse** is a popular winter sports centre. It is equipped with a selection of ski and chair lifts, has a school of cross-country skiing and is famous for its cheese. The main hotel — the Vallées et sa Residence — in the Rue Claudel, ☎ 29 25 41 89 is large and comfortable with a covered swimming pool, tennis in the grounds and ample parking space for cars.

There is no particularly quick or easy way of getting from La Bresse to **St-Maurice-sur-Moselle** on the N66, about 7km (4 miles) from the source of the river in the shadow of the Ballon d'Alsace. It prides itself on being a resort for all seasons and hardly misses a trick as far as outdoor activities are concerned. Summer visitors can play tennis and *boules* and there is a municipal swimming pool as well as a riding centre that provides horses and ponies for trips of anything from a few hours to several days. Trout fishermen can try their luck in a variety of different streams once they have obtained the necessary licence, while serious hikers and holidaymakers out for a gentle stroll have a choice of marked footpaths that wander off in all directions. In winter there are ski runs to suit all comers, tuition is available and excursions are planned using the well-defined *randonnées de ski*. In addition to a sprinkling of rather Alpine-like hotels there is a three star campsite which is open throughout the year. From St-Maurice-sur-Moselle the N66 follows the Moselle Valley northwards to pause at Remiremont where it joins the main road to Épinal.

North of Épinal, also in the valley of the Moselle, **Charmes** was where Richelieu and Charles IV, Duc de Lorraine, signed a treaty which transferred Nancy to France in 1633. Nearly three centuries later French troops under General Castelnau were victorious in a battle known as the 'Trouée de Charmes' in 1914 but 30 years on the Germans got their own back by setting fire to the town as their armies retreated towards Mulhouse and the Rhine. With the end of the War

Typical town house in the Lorraine area

in Europe Charmes was rebuilt rather than restored and therefore has little to detain even the most ardent sightseer.

Fortunately Charmes is only 17km (11 miles) via the D55 from **Mirecourt** where there is an imposing covered market, complete with arcades and two matching square towers, dating from 1617. The church of Notre-Dame and the Chapelle de la Oultre are considerably older although they were both added to and improved upon in the sixteenth and seventeenth centuries. The town's less publicised claims to fame are lacemaking and embroidery and its long association with families engaged in making traditional musical instruments. The Musée de Mirecourt traces the history of stringed instruments including violins and violas with names such as Cognier and Terrier or Morizot, mandolins produced by the brothers Gérome and guitars bearing the Pagès hallmark. It has been said that Mirecourt smells of wood and glue and this is certainly true of the sawmill-workshop of Henry Miller, where visitors can make an appointment to see the craftsmen at work by telephoning 29 37 10 70.

The D429 links Mirecourt with **Vittel**, a busy spa town about 23km (14 miles) to the south-west. It divides its time between exporting bottled water and entertaining visitors who arrive in search of a cure for arthritis, gout, migraine and a wide range of other ailments. At least one of the hotels, the Bellevue in the Avenue Châtillon, ☎ 29 08 07 98 makes special provision for disabled guests. The thermal baths are located in a large attractive park where numerous concerts are held during the season. There are plenty of things to do for patients who are making a good recovery or for holidaymakers who simply want to relax and enjoy themselves. They can walk or swim, play tennis or golf, watch polo, go to the races, visit the nearby flying club and try their luck at the casino.

Vittel's nearest neighbour is **Contrexéville**, a spa of comparable size which offers an equally wide range of treatments and nearly as many entertainments but does rather better in the way of hotels. The most up-market of these are the Cosmos in the Rue Metz, ☎ 29 08 15 90, near the casino, and the Grand Hôtel Établissement, ☎ 29 08 17 30 but there are several other quite adequate versions to choose from, although not necessarily at appreciably lower prices. The town prides itself on being a good centre for excursions into the surrounding countryside. An obvious example is the Lac de la Folie, 1½km (1 mile) to the north-west, which provides opportunities for fishing or swimming but, so far, no boating. Meanwhile Bulgnéville, on the edge of the forest, has a very viewable old church and the Fontaine des Curtilles, carefully restored in 1750. In the opposite direction **Darney**, on the D164 in the direction of Bains-les-Bains, was where the Allies proclaimed the independence of Czechoslovakia in 1918. The ceremony was attended by Eduard Benes, the new Republic's first foreign minister who succeeded Masaryk as President in 1935. The occasion is recalled in the small Musée Tchécoslovaque (Czechoslovak Museum), housed in the Hôtel de Ville.

The D164 from Contrexéville crosses the *autoroute* just beyond Bulgnéville and continues on its way through pleasant if rather unspectacular country to **Neufchâteau**. Here it meets up with several other main roads that converge on the town from at least five different directions, one of which keeps in touch with Épinal 75km (46 miles) away. In the olden days Neufchâteau was a Roman settlement but they obviously did not consider it important enough to build anything of lasting significance. Nevertheless it survived and prospered, building the Église St-Christophe in 1100 and the Église St-Nicolas shortly afterwards. Both these churches were added to as time went by, the former acquiring a nice line in fonts and a Louis XV pulpit, while the latter collected a variety of statues including a famous fifteenth-century polychrome referred to simply as the Groupe en Pierre.

The town is sadly lacking in towers and ramparts despite the fact that it was heavily fortified in the Middle Ages. The château and all its defences were destroyed on the orders of Cardinal Richelieu, who had a habit of eliminating anyone who took part in a revolt or thwarted him in some other way. However the Hôtel de Ville was allowed to keep its Renaissance doorway and an eyecatching staircase that is well worth seeing. Proof that the Romans did spend some time in the area can be found at **Grand**, within easy reach of Neufchâteau through either Liffol-le-Grand or Midrevaux. Apart from its Gallo-Roman remains there is a local museum full of mosaics which are considered by some people to be the most important collection in the region to the west of the Alps. Enquire at the Mairie for opening times.

It is doubtful if many people would ever have heard of **Domrémy-la-Pucelle**, let alone visited this all-but-non-existent little hamlet, if Joan of Arc had not been born there on Twelfth Night in 1412. As it is, tourists arrive in their hundreds to inspect the typical peasant's cottage where she was brought up by her parents, Isabelle Romée and Jacques d'Arc. It is an extremely modest little stone building with bare walls, a sloping roof and absolutely nothing inside, although it was embellished some time later with a coat-of-arms, an appropriate inscription and a small statue over the door. To the left of the cottage is a miniscule museum devoted almost exclusively to the girl who heard voices and left her spinning wheel to inspire both the Dauphin and the French troops who were fighting against the combined forces of England and Burgundy. Nearby is the village church which has changed very little since Joan of Arc was christened in the twelfth-century font under the watchful eye of the statue of Ste-Marguerite, although the stained glass windows were added a good deal later.

About 1½km (1 mile) away, in the Chenu Woods, work started in 1881 on building the Basilica du Bois-Chenu, marking one of the places where Joan of Arc said she received her instructions from Ste-Catherine, Ste-Marguerite and St-Michel. The church was consecrated 45 years later, after St Joan had been canonised in Rome on 16 May 1920. The interior is decorated with frescoes by Lionel Royer tracing the life of the peasant girl who raised the siege of Orleans, was captured by the Burgundians, sold to the English, tried for heresy and witchcraft and burned in the market place at Rouen, all before she was twenty years old.

From Domrémy-la-Pucelle the D19 makes its way through a quartet of small villages to join the N74 a few kilometres south of Colombey-les-Belles. Thereafter it runs parallel with the *autoroute* to Toul, leaving the D974 to negotiate the last 32km (20 miles) to Nancy. Alternatively, some people who take part in the annual pilgrimage to the Basilica du Bois-Chenu prefer to leave for the north along the D964, following in the steps of St Joan to Vaucouleurs, where she made her first contact with a small troop of French soldiers on her way to find the Dauphin and see him crowned in Reims.

Additional Information

Places to Visit

MEUSE

Bar-le-Duc
Église Notre-Dame
Rue Jeanne d'Arc
Closed Sunday and holiday afternoons.

Musée Barrois
Rue du Baile
Open: afternoons June to mid-September. Wednesday, Saturday and Sunday afternoons mid-September to May. Closed Tuesdays and holidays.

Commercy
Château
Avenue Stanislas
Open: for guided tours at 3pm mid-July to end of August. Also at 4.30pm on Sundays and holidays. Otherwise by request. Closed Tuesdays.
☎ 91 02 18

Hattonchâtel
Château
Guided tours each morning and afternoon.

Louppy-sur-Loison
Château
Guided tours afternoons only July to September. Closed Mondays and the rest of the year.

Montmédy
Ramparts
Open: all day April to September.
Mornings and afternoons February,
March and October. Otherwise on
request.
☎ 80 11 89

Stenay
Musée
On the outskirts
Open: mornings and afternoons
July and August. Saturday and
Sunday morning and afternoon
only May and June.

Vaucouleurs
Chapelle Castrale
Off the Rue de l'Observatoire
Open: all day.

Musée Municipal
In the town hall
Open: mornings and afternoons
mid-June to mid-September.
Closed Tuesdays.

Verdun
Hôtel de la Princerie Musée
Off the Place Maginot
Open: mornings and afternoons
from Easter to the end of September. Closed Tuesdays.

Monument de la Victoire
Can be visited during the season.
Enquire at the tourist office if
necessary.

Souterrains de la Citadelle
Visit in the mornings and afternoons. Closed from mid-December
to mid-January.

*Mémorial-Musée de la Bataille de
    Verdun*
In the battle area to the north-east.
Open: mornings and afternoons.
Closed mid-December to mid-
January.

MEURTHE-ET-MOSELLE

Baccarat
Musée du Cristal
In the château at the main crossroads
Open: mornings and afternoons
mid-July to mid-September. Closed
Tuesday mornings and Sundays.
Afternoons only mid-June to mid-
July and second half of September.
Saturday and Sunday afternoons
May to mid-June. Closed for the
remainder of the year.

Cons-la-Grandville
Château
Guided tours from mid-July to the
end of August.

Fermont
Fort
Open: for guided tours each afternoon from April to September. Saturday and Sunday afternoons during October. Saturday afternoons
only during the rest of the year.

Fléville
Château
Open: for guided tours afternoons
only July and August. Sunday and
holiday afternoons only April to
June, September and October.

Haroué
Château
Open: for guided tours afternoons
only from April to mid-November.

Haye
Musée de l'Aéronautique
Parc de la Forêt de Haye
Open: Saturday afternoons and
Sundays January to August.

Musée de l'Auto
Open: Wednesday, Saturday and
Sunday afternoons March to mid-
November.

Lunéville

Château
Museum open mornings and afternoons. Closed Tuesdays. Also 'Son et Lumiere le Grand Carrousel' at 9.30pm Fridays, Saturdays and Sundays July and August. 10.30pm for the first half of September.

Musée de la Moto et du Vélo
Open: mornings and afternoons. Closed Mondays.

Nancy

Cristalleries Daum
Rue des Cristalleries
Open: weekday mornings and Saturday mornings and afternoons. Closed Sundays.

Église et Couvent des Cordeliers
On the Grande-Rue
Open: mornings and afternoons. Closed Mondays, 1 January, Easter, All Saints' Day and Christmas.

Hôtel de Ville
Open: during business hours.

Jardin Botanique du Montet
In Vandoeuvre, off the Avenue Général Leclerc
Open: in the afternoons. Closed Mondays and Tuesdays.

Jardin Botanique Ste-Catherine
Off the Rue Ste-Catherine
Open: daily but closed on Sunday mornings.

Musée des Beaux-Arts
On the Place Stanislas
Open: mornings and afternoons. Closed Monday mornings, Tuesdays and holidays.

Musée de l'École de Nancy
Rue Sergent-Blandan
Open: mornings and afternoons. Closed Tuesdays, 1 January, Easter, 1 May, 14 July, All Saints Day and Christmas.

Musée de l'Histoire du Fer
Jarville-la-Maigrange
Open: most mornings and afternoons. Closing times vary slightly so enquire from the tourist office.

Musée de Zoologie
Jardin Botanique Ste-Catherine
Open: afternoons only. Closed Tuesdays except during school holidays.

Palais Ducal and Musée Historique Lorraine
In the Grande-Rue
Open: mornings and afternoons. Closed Tuesdays.

Porte de la Craffe
Rue de la Craffe
Open: mornings and afternoons mid-June to August. Closed Tuesdays.

Pont-à-Mousson

Abbaye des Prémontrés
Closed late December and early January. For exact times enquire from the Syndicat d'Initiative.

Hôtel de Ville
Open: during business hours.

Sion

Musée Archéologique et Missionnaire
Open: from Easter to October.

Toul

Église St-Gengoult
Only open on Sundays. To visit at other times enquire from the presbytery.
☎ 343 04 52

MOSELLE

Gravelotte

Musée de la Guerre
Open: mornings and afternoons.

Hartzviller

Cristallerie de Hartzviller
10km (6 miles) to the south on the D44
Open: mornings and afternoons when the factory is open.

Marsal

Maison du Sel
Near the Porte de France
Open: mornings and afternoons
Tuesdays, Thursdays, Fridays and
Saturdays (but afternoons only
Mondays, Wednesdays and
Sundays) from February to
December. Saturday afternoons
only in January. Closed 1 January,
Good Friday, 1 May, Christmas
and Boxing Day.

Metz

Ancien Couvent des Récollets
Behind the hospital
Open: mornings and afternoons.
Closed Saturday afternoon,
Sundays and holidays.

Cathedral Crypt
Open: mornings and afternoons
Monday to Saturday. Closed
Sunday mornings and holidays.

Cathedral Treasure
Open: every afternoon. Closed on
religious holidays.

Chapelle des Templiers
Off the Esplanade
Open: mornings and afternoons in
summer. At other times enquire at
the Bureaux du Génie opposite the
chapel.

Église St Maximin
Rue Mazelle
Closed Thursdays.

Église St-Vincent
Enquire at No 6, Rue St-Vincent

Musée d'Art et d'Histoire
Rue Chanoine-Collin
Open: mornings and afternoons.
Closed Tuesdays.

Phalsbourg

Musée Municipal
In the Hôtel de Ville
Open: mornings and afternoons

Wednesdays and Saturdays.
Afternoons only Mondays,
Tuesdays, Thursdays and Fridays.
Mornings only on Sundays and
holidays. Closed November to
mid-March.

Sarrebourg

Chapelle des Cordeliers
Off the Grand Rue
Open: mornings and afternoons.
Closed Sundays except during July
and August, also on Mondays and
holidays.

Domaine Gallo-Roman de St-Ulrich
4km (2 miles) to the north-west
towards Haut-Clocher
Open: 4-5pm Sundays and
holidays from Easter to mid-
September. Otherwise enquire at
the Auberge St-Ulrich.

Musée du Pays de Sarrebourg
Avenue de France
Open: mornings and afternoons.
Closed Sunday except during July
and August and also on Tuesdays
and holidays.

Sarreguemines

Musée Céramique
Rue Poincaré
Open: mornings and afternoons.
Closed Tuesdays and holidays.

Thionville

Château de la Grange
On the outskirts off the N53.
Guided tours in the afternoon on
Saturdays, Sundays and holidays.

Musée d'Archéologie et d'Histoire
In the Tour aux Puces on the Quai
    Marchal
Open: afternoons only. Closed
Mondays and holidays.

Walibi-Schtroumpf

Amusement park on the N52
Open: 10am-6pm daily (10am-7pm

Sundays and holidays) late April to end of June. 10am-7pm daily July to early September. 10am-6pm Wednesdays, Saturdays and Sundays for the rest of September. Closed October to late April.

VOSGES

Darney
Musée Tchécoslovaque
In the Hôtel de Ville
Open: during working hours.

Domrémy-la-Pucelle
Joan of Arc's Birthplace and Museum
Open: mornings and afternoons. Closed Tuesdays from mid-October to March.

Épinal
Imagerie Pellerin
Off the Quay de Dogneville
Guided tours mornings and afternoons. Afternoons only Sundays and holidays.

Musée des Vosges et de l'Imagerie
Place Lagarde on the island
Open: mornings and afternoons. Closed on Tuesdays, 1 January, 1 May, 1 November and 25 December.

Étival-Clairefontaine
Church closed on Sundays.

Mirecourt
Chapelle de la Oultre
Near the Pont St-Vincent
If closed enquire from the warden in the Place de la Chapelle.

Musée de Mirecourt
Enquire at the Syndicat d'Initiative de Mirecourt, in the Mairie. Rue du Gal-Leclerc ☎ 29 37 05 22

La Moineaudiere
Musée
In the hotel on the Route du Valtin near Xonrupt-Longemer

Open: 9am-12noon and 2-6.30pm daily. Closed Mondays except during school holidays. Also one week in March and throughout November.

Neufchâteau
Hôtel de Ville
Rue St Jean
Open: during office hours.

Église St-Christophe
Rue de la Comédie
Closed on Sundays.

Église St-Nicolas
Rue St Nicolas
If closed enquire from the priest, 7 Rue de la Comédie. Usually open on summer afternoons.

Plombières-les-Bains
Bain Stanislas
Rue Stanislas
Open: May to September. Closed on Sundays.

Musée Louis-Français
Avenue Louis-Français
Open: afternoons May to September. Closed Tuesdays, Whit Sunday, 14 July and 15 August.

Poussay
Henry Miller workshop
☎ 29 37 10 70 to arrange a visit.

Remiremont
Municipal Museums
Rue Charles de Gaulle and Rue Genéral Humbert
Both open mornings and afternoons. Closed Tuesday, some public holidays and Sundays from mid-January to end of February.

La Rochère
Glass Factory, including Art Gallery
Passavant-la-Rochère
Workshops open 2.30-5.30pm on weekdays May to July and during September. Closed Sundays and holidays.

Art Gallery and Glass Exhibition
Open: 2.30-6pm daily from May to
September.

St-Dié
Bibliothèque
Behind the cathedral
Open: mornings and afternoons.
Closed Sundays, Mondays and
some public holidays.

Église de Notre-Dame-de-Galilée
Adjoining the cathedral
Often closed except on holidays.
Enquire at the cathedral or the
Tourist Office.

Musée Municipal
Beside the cathedral
Open: mornings and afternoons.
Closed Mondays and public holidays.

Senones
Maison Abbatiale
Near the church
Closed on Sundays.
Steam train to Étival. Saturdays,
Sundays and holidays May to mid-
September.

Steam Train To Senones
Runs on Saturdays, Sundays and
holidays May to mid-September.
For information and reservations
telephone 57 60 32.

Vittel
*Usine d'Embouteillage (Bottled Water
Factory)*
Tours can be arranged, mornings
and afternoons mid-April to mid-
September. Closed Saturdays,
Sundays and public holidays.

Tourist Information Centres
MEUSE
Bar-le-Duc
Office de Tourisme
Rue Lapique
☎ 29 79 11 13

Montmédy
Office de Tourisme
Ville Haute
Open: February to October.
☎ 29 80 15 90

St-Mihiel
Syndicat d'Initiative
Place Halles
Open: Easter to October.
☎ 29 89 04 50

Verdun
Office de Tourisme
Place Nation
Open: May to mid-September.
☎ 29 84 18 85

MEURTHE-ET-MOSELLE
Baccarat
Syndicat d'Initiative
Place Arcades
Open: June to September.
☎ 83 75 13 37

Longwy
Syndicat d'Initiative
Gare Routière
Closed in the mornings.
☎ 82 24 27 17

Lunéville
Office de Tourisme
In the château
☎ 83 74 06 55

Nancy
Office de Tourisme and Accueil de
France
Place Stanislas
☎ 83 35 22 41

Pont-à-Mousson
Syndicat d'Initiative
Place Duroc
☎ 83 81 06 90

Toul
Syndicat d'Initiative
Parvis Cathédrale
☎ 83 64 11 69

Moselle
Bitche
Office de Tourisme
In the Mairie
☎ 87 96 00 13

Dabo
Syndicat d'Initiative
Place de l'Église
Open: July and August.
☎ 87 07 47 51

Metz
Office de Tourisme and Accueil de
France
Place d'Armes
☎ 87 75 65 21

At the station
☎ 87 65 76 69

Phalsbourg
Syndicat d'Initiative
Hôtel de Ville
Open: May to October.
☎ 87 24 12 26

Sarrebourg
Office de Tourisme
Chapelle des Cordeliers
☎ 87 03 11 82

Sarreguemines
Office de Tourisme
Rue Maire Massing
☎ 87 98 80 81

Thionville
Office de Tourisme
Rue Vieux-Collège
☎ 82 53 33 18

Walibi-Schtroumpf
Syndicat d'Initiative d'Hagondange
☎ 87 70 35 27

Office de Tourisme d'Amneville
☎ 87 70 10 40, or the park itself
☎ 87 51 73 90

VOSGES

Épinal
Office de Tourisme
Rue Comédie
☎ 29 82 53 32

Gérardmer
Office de Tourisme
Place Déportés
☎ 29 63 08 74

Neufchâteau
Syndicat d'Initiative
In the Mairie
☎ 29 94 14 75

Plombières-les-Bains
Office de Tourisme
Rue Stanislas
Open: May to September.
☎ 29 66 01 30

Remiremont
Syndicat d'Initiative
Place H. Utard
Closed in the mornings out of
season.
☎ 29 62 23 70

St-Dié
Office de Tourisme
Rue Thiers
☎ 29 55 17 62

St-Maurice-sur-Moselle
Syndicat d'Initiative
In the Mairie
☎ 29 25 11 21

Chalet du Syndicat d'Initiative
Place du 2 October
Open: in July and August
☎ 29 25 12 34

Vittel
Syndicat d'Initiative
Rue de Verdun
☎ 29 08 42 03

Also Palais des Congrès
Open: May to September.
☎ 29 08 12 72

3

ALSACE

A lsace consists of two *départements* of more or less comparable size. Bas-Rhin, in the north, is partly enclosed by Germany and includes Strasbourg, the provincial capital, while Haut-Rhin follows the River Rhine down to Switzerland and lays claim to Grand Ballon, at 1,424m (4,671ft) the highest peak in the region.

Either *département* can be reached quite easily by air, rail or road. Strasbourg has a busy international airport but it is also possible to fly to Colmar or Mulhouse which shares its airport with Basle on the other side of the river. For anyone who prefers to travel by train there are two main routes from Paris, both of them varied and enjoyable. The shorter one runs through champagne country, pausing at Châlons-sur-Marne, calls at Nancy in Lorraine and then makes a B-line for Strasbourg. The southerly option is rather more leisurely. It heads for Chaumont before threading its way through the Vosges mountains to Mulhouse where it changes direction, turning north to Colmar which is generally considered to be the prettiest town in Alsace. From there it is virtually a straight run across the Plaine d'Alsace to Strasbourg. Self-drive cars can be hired in the larger centres whereas motorail facilities are available to Strasbourg and Mulhouse for drivers who would rather take their own vehicles.

The best way to explore Alsace is undoubtedly by car and, for anyone who enjoys driving, several options are open from the Channel coast to Strasbourg, a distance by the most direct route of about 640km (400 miles). It is possible to use motorways for the entire journey, taking the A26 from Calais to Reims and then the A4 — the Autoroute de l'Est — past Verdun and Metz to Strasbourg. Alternatively there are any number of other routes available, using major roads and calling at a variety of interesting places along the way. If time is no object the entire trip to any part of the region can be done by selecting a series of secondary roads and an occasional byway.

Once in Alsace, Mulhouse offers a choice of *autoroutes* — north to Colmar, eastwards across the Rhine into Germany, due south through Basle for a tour of Switzerland or south-west on the A36. This links up with the Autoroute du Soleil in Burgundy between Dijon and Beaune which follows the Rhine Valley down to the Mediterranean. Apart from a comprehensive network of major roads Alsace also offers a selection of well-defined routes that enable visitors to choose exactly the type of local attractions that appeal to them. Scenically the most impressive is the mountain road known as the Route de Crêtes. It begins about 40km (25 miles) south-west of Strasbourg, near Obernai, and wends its way round Mont Ste-Odile, past the Black Lake and the White Lake and over some memorable passes like the Col de la Schlucht, commanding a series of extensive views across the Plaine d'Alsace to the Black Forest. Thereafter it drops down gradually towards Thann and Mulhouse.

The Route du Vin is no less fascinating. It wanders effortlessly for 120km (75 miles) from Marlenheim southwards through the foothills of the Vosges, past ruined castles and photogenic little towns and villages surrounded by vineyards. Some were fortified in days gone by while others are known for their elderly churches, half-timbered houses, historical associations or other individual attractions. The oldest of the ubiquitous vineyards is said to be at Wettolsheim, near Colmar, dating back to the time of the Romans. Other, less frequented excursions include the Route du Fromage, or Cheese Road, west of Munster where the small country inns serve Munster cheese in addition to a number of other specialities. The nearby Route de Cinq Châteaux numbers five castles, two of them in ruins, among its main attractions, leaving the Routes de la Carpe Frite a free hand in the Sundgau area between Mulhouse and the Jura mountains. This is a pleasant, rather undemanding part of the country, peppered with small communities, an occasional reminder of its past history and plenty of taverns renowned for their fried fish.

The north of the province also has its specially marked tourist routes such as the Route des Villages Pittoresque (Road of the Picturesque Villages) south of Wissembourg and the Route des Châteaux Forts which provides access to about ten fortified castles, the majority of them little more than ruins. Apart from these well-defined routes Alsace has an excellent network of main and secondary roads augmented by lanes and byways that seldom deteriorate into cart tracks. Horses and bicycles are available for excursions into the countryside and there are several hundred miles of marked footpaths for visitors who prefer to do their exploring on foot. Nearly

Musée Alsacien
Musée Historique

GERMANY

Musée Westercamp

Niedersteinbach

Wissembourg

D3

Niederbronn-les-Bains

D28

Hunspach

D919

N61

D9

N62

Betschdorf

N63

La Petite Pierre

D919

Sessenheim

Musée du Sceau Alsacien

Château

A4

Haguenau

D300

D421

Saverne

N4

Château
Jardin Botanique

Strasbourg

ALSACE

Molsheim

D392

Rosheim

Obernai

Mont Ste Odile

BAS-RHIN

Danbach-la-Vine

D424

N422

N83

D5

Bibliothèque
Humaniste

Sélestat

Musée d'Unterlinden

Musée Bartholdi

N59

D416

Ste-Marie-aux-Mines

Ribeauvillé

D468

Rhin

N415

Kintzheim

Kaysersberg
Ammerschwihr

Colmar

D417

N83

N415

Musée Albert Schweitzer

Musée Communal

HAUT-

Eguisheim

Neuf-Brisach

Rouffach

RHIN

Freiburg

Guebwiller

N66

A35

GERMANY

St-Amarin

Cernay

Ensisheim

Thann

Musée de l'Automobile

Musée Français du Chenin de Fer

Musée Historique

Musée de l'Impressionsur Étoffes

Musée des
Amis de Thann

Mulhouse

A36

Altkirch

D419

Basel

Musée
Sundgauvien

every town and village has its own selected paths covering anything from 16km to 40km (10 to 25 miles) and one or two even arrange organised walks to places of interest in the vicinity. These vary from one centre to another in many respects, among the more unusual suggestions being the Vita Course Parcours, or Health Walk, from Colmar and the specially designed sportive path at Barr. Most of the towns and larger villages have an *auberge*, a *logi* or a modest inn where it is possible to find a bed for the night. However many people find it more convenient to choose a comfortable hotel in one of the main centres and then make leisurely day trips from there, as and when the spirit moves them and the weather is fine. This presents very few difficulties because the average outing seldom involves a round trip of more than 161km (100 miles). Another advantage of having a base in one of the major towns is that guided tours by coach are available to many leading places of interest, augmented by other excursions during the tourist season.

BAS-RHIN

Visitors in search of first class accommodation, memorable food and wine and a large selection of entertainments and other attractions need look no further than **Strasbourg**. The city is acutely aware of its obligations as a Euro-Capital, especially as it also caters for the needs   ❋

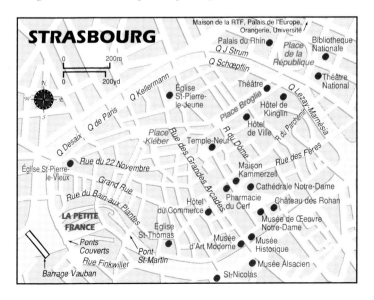

of delegates to the Council of Europe, and members of the European Parliament, the Court of Human Rights and the European Science Foundation, as well as visitors to whom money is no object. At the same time it makes ample provision for ordinary holidaymakers with plenty of less expensive hotels and restaurants scattered throughout the city and in several towns and villages in the immediate vicinity. In addition, special facilities are available for people in search of a particular type of holiday which may be anything from exploring the waterways by boat, touring the Bas-Rhin on horseback, studying the local arts and traditions or even inspecting the countryside from a hot-air balloon.

With so many hotels to choose from, including a number that belong to well-known chains such as the Hilton, Holiday Inn, Sofitel and Novotel, it is difficult to mention a mere handful, especially as there are many others which are just as convenient for sightseers. For example, the popular Nouvel Hôtel Maison Rouge, 4 Rue des Francs-Bourgeois, ☎ 88 32 08 60, is within a stone's throw of the Place Kléber and only a few blocks from the cathedral. It has a bar and a breakfast room but no restaurant and there is parking for the car quite close by. Much the same applies to the Hôtel des Rohan, 17 Rue Maroquin, ☎ 88 32 85 11, a smaller family hotel in a cobbled pedestrian area even closer to the cathedral. Finding somewhere for lunch or dinner is very simple because there is no shortage of restaurants in Strasbourg and one can eat well almost anywhere in the city. In the old quarter they include the excellent but predictably expensive Crocodile in the Rue Outre, leading off the Place Kleber, and the much cheaper L'Ancienne Douane in the Rue Douane which has a terrace overlooking the River Ill near the Musée d'Art Moderne. Slightly further afield, on the Avenue de la Liberte, the Hôtel Le Régent Contades, ☎ 88 36 26 26, is a nineteenth-century mansion beside the river which offers its guests a special inclusive holiday. Among the attractions listed are the hotel's various leisure facilities, a trip round the city by boat and golf — for handicap players only — at the 18-hole Kempferhof course near Plobsheim on the D468 a few kilometres to the south.

Entertainments in Strasbourg tend to be sophisticated rather than folksy, personified by the International Music Festival in June. The headquarters of the Opéra du Rhin are in the Place de Broglie while the Europa Cantat in the Rue des Balayeurs arranges lyrical and choral concerts at quite frequent intervals. Ancient music is kept very much alive by the Association pour la Musique sur Instruments Anciens which not only organises concerts and conferences but also supervises training sessions, while the so-called Music of Today has its own International Festival in late September or early October. Strasbourg also has a National Theatre, holds an important European Fair at the beginning of September and pulls out all the stops in the Place de Broglie 3 months later with its Christmas decorations.

On a more energetic note there are sports stadia, Olympic swimming pools, indoor and outdoor tennis courts, a skating rink near the Palais des Congrés and facilities for golf, sailing, riding and fishing within easy reach of the city. Flying and gliding lessons can be arranged through the local aero clubs whereas the Office Départemental du Tourisme du Bas-Rhin has all the necessary information concerning theme holidays, which may be anything from cooking or painting to wine tasting or exploring the surrounding area on foot.

Although Strasbourg has a tendency to sprawl in all directions, with outlying suburbs that are as devoid of interest as those of any other provincial capital, most of its principal attractions are contained in a relatively small area in the middle, completely surrounded by water. For the first-time visitor the best way to become at least partly orientated is to take a trip on one of the pleasure boats through the picturesque canals, which are many and varied, or else opt for a guided tour on the mini-train that caters almost exclusively for sightseers. Failing that, it is better to take a taxi than attempt to drive round by car because parking is rather restricted and most of the allotted spaces are usually full. Having once located the cathedral, the Place Kléber, La Petite France and the Place de la République across the water from the Place de Broglie, it is time to change into comfortable shoes, obtain a map from the tourist office or bookshop and set off for the nearest place of interest.

To appreciate all the different sights it helps to know a little about the history of this ancient town which started life as a village inhabited mainly by hunters and fishermen until the Romans established a small settlement there and called it *Argentoratum*. Before long this modest outpost had grown into a thriving centre, located strategically at the crossroads of Europe, which suggested another change of name, this time to *Strateburgum*, which meant quite literally the Town of the Roads. As was only to be expected, such a rich prize lying in the path of each subsequent invader resulted in a steady stream of misfortunes, some more disastrous than others. It was constantly being bombarded, captured, burnt and pillaged, resulting in plague and pestilence, only to be rebuilt before history repeated itself. The city changed hands with monotonous regularity until it was finally returned to France at the end of World War II.

Sandwiched in between these periods of trial and tribulation

Sightseeing around the city of Strasbourg by train

The delightful old houses that characterise La Petite France, once the home of fishermen, tanners and millers, Strasbourg

Strasbourg enjoyed both peace and prosperity and made the most of them to score some notable successes. Following the death of Charlemagne feuds broke out between younger members of his family, all of whom wanted the lion's share of his vast empire. Eventually, in AD842 the town was the setting for a reconciliation between Charles and Louis, the sons of Louis le Débonnaire, which satisfied both of them and is known as the Serment de Strasbourg. A good deal later Johann Gutenberg, who invented printing from movable type, did much of the ground work while he was living in the city in the early fifteenth century. The first university was founded in 1567, slightly more than 200 years before Goethe enrolled as a student, whereas the cathedral had been completely restored and renovated before it received a visit from Marie Antoinette in 1770 on her way to marry Louis XVI. Two years later Rouget de Lisle was stationed in Strasbourg when he composed the *Battle Hymn of the Army of the Rhine*. It was exactly suited to the mood of the revolutionaries who adopted it at roughly the same time as they sent the royal couple to the guillotine, but retitled it *La Marseillaise*. Over the years Strasbourg had established an enviable reputation for outstanding food and wine and this still applies in the city as it does in many towns and villages throughout Alsace.

In view of its extremely turbulent history Strasbourg has managed to preserve quite a few reminders of the past, foremost among them being the **Cathédrale Notre-Dame**, built on the site of the ancient temple of Hercules. This large pink sandstone church dates back to the twelfth century, its Romanesque predecessor having been burned down shortly after St Bernard celebrated mass there. It was designed along Gothic lines and given its extravagantly decorated façade by Erwin de Steinbach, who managed to cram a great many biblical events into a relatively confined space. Everyone who was anyone in the Old Testament seems to be gathered round the main door, from Adam and Eve and Cain and Abel to Abraham, Jacob, Samson and Solomon, seated on his throne all alone. Apart from two statues of the Virgin and Child, the life of Christ is restricted mainly to the period between the Entry into Jerusalem and the Ascension. Meanwhile, the door on the right is enlivened by the parable of the Wise and Foolish Virgins, although the statues of the seducer tempting a hopeful-looking young woman with an apple are copies of the originals which are preserved in the Musée de l'Œuvre Notre-Dame. Towering more than 122m (400ft) above the façade, with its large and beautiful rose window, the famous steeple was added in 1439 and can be climbed by anyone with enough energy to attempt 328 steps.

The interior of the Cathédrale Notre-Dame is equally impressive with its long nave, splendid stained glass windows from the twelfth, thirteenth and fourteenth centuries, original pulpit, statues and fascinating astronomical clock. This comparative newcomer, which for some reason is always half an hour behind everyone else, marks the days of the week with pagan gods and goddesses. Monday belongs to Diana, Tuesday to Mars and so on, with Mercury, Jupiter, Venus and Saturn, while Apollo brings up the rear on Sunday. The passage of time is marked in quarters by Infancy, Adolescence, Maturity and Old Age. Elsewhere there are some fine seventeenth-century tapestries, steps down to the ancient crypt and a stained glass window added in 1956 to commemorate the establishment of important European institutions in the city.

Several historic buildings are situated within sight of the cathedral, among them the **Pharmacie du Cerf**, opposite the main door, which was built in 1268 and is said to be the oldest pharmacy in France. It has a diagonal view of the somewhat younger Maison Kammerzell, decorated with frescoes and wood carving, which was completely restored in 1954 and is now an up-market restaurant. Meanwhile, on the far side of the Place de la Cathédrale, the **Musée de l'Œuvre Notre-Dame** consists of a group of elderly buildings linked by their respective courtyards, although part of it was destroyed during an aerial bombardment in 1944. The museum concerns itself with the history of Strasbourg in general and the history of the cathedral in particular. It looks back over its shoulder to Roman times with some not very inspiring sculptures and displays an occasional window from the early church. Then there are architectural drawings on parchment which were used in the building of the present cathedral in addition to some tapestries, medieval gold and silver work, paintings and seventeenth-century costumes.

Just across the Rue de Rohan, facing on to the Place du Château, the opulent **Château des Rohan** was built in 1704 as a palace for Cardinal Armand de Rohan-Soubise, the Prince-Bishop of Strasbourg, and his successors. Despite its high-ranking ecclesiastical background the château is more frequently associated with Louis de Rohan who, with Jeanne de la Motte, was responsible for the infamous affair of Marie-Antoinette's diamond necklace. The queen had refused to buy it on the grounds that it was too expensive but Rohan pretended to be acting for her and the jeweller handed it over to La Motte, under the impression that she was the queen. The bill was paid from official funds before the plot was discovered and the two adventurers punished, but Marie-Antoinette was so unpopular by that time that very few people were willing to give her the benefit of the doubt. Nowadays the château is home to three of the city's leading museums, while at the same time preserving some of the original state apartments.

The **Musée des Beaux Arts** concentrates mainly on paintings with works by such artists as Rubens, Zurbarán, Van Dyke and Goya as well as some interesting examples from the Middle Ages. There is also the Galerie Alsacienne, reserved for local artists from 1850 onwards. The **Musée des Arts Décoratifs** is more interested in ceramics of every description and claims to have one of the most outstanding collections in France. There is some beautiful porcelain that was made in Strasbourg during the eighteenth century as well as gold and silver work, decorative flowers and animals and some rather nice pieces of furniture. Meanwhile, the **Musée Archéologique** delves back into pre-history with a varied assortment of bits and pieces ranging from flints, axeheads and primitive tools to pieces of pottery, weapons and jewellery. Also on display are relics from the days of the Romans and the Franks that have been discovered at several places in the city and the surrounding region.

For anyone with an insatiable appetite for information there are three other interesting museums nearby, more or less grouped around the Pont de Corbeau. This is another survivor from the past, known originally as the Pont des Supplices, where the torture in question consisted of locking up murderers in iron cages, especially those who killed children or old people, and plunging them into the river to drown. The **Musée Historique**, on the Place de la Grande-Boucherie, is somewhat preoccupied with military matters and is crammed with uniforms, weapons and armaments, including cannons, while still finding space for a colourful array of miniature soldiers. In addition there are maps and models, documents, engravings and other exhibits in the section devoted to the history of the city. The **Musée Alsacien**, on the other side of the river, is less inclined to specialise, dividing its attention more or less equally between traditional costumes and local crafts, various occupations such as agriculture, milling and wine making, the study of pills and potions and items of sacred art. The **Musée d'Art Moderne**, in the old Customs House, is only concerned with the nineteenth and twentieth centuries, concentrating on Impressionists like Renoir, Monet and Pissaro as well as contemporary stained glass.

A few blocks up river, the **Église St-Thomas** on the Rue Martin-Luther, is worth visiting to see the Mausoleé du Maréchal de Saxe with its attendant lion representing Holland, a leopard personifying England and an Austrian eagle. Other things to look out for are the twelfth-century tomb of Bishop Adeloch, tucked away in its own little chapel, and the eighteenth-century organ. Beyond the church a path beside the river leads to the Port St-Martin, known particularly for its view over the ancient quarter of Bain-aux-Plantes. This was always a busy area set about with mills and tanneries, the canals controlled by lock-keepers and the streets lined with picturesque medieval houses. The Rue du Bains-aux-Plantes leads in due course to La Petite France where a trio of towers interspersed with bridges mark the line of the ancient ramparts. Facing them is the **Barrage Vauban** which was built to control the river and commands an even more attractive view.

Leaving behind the canals and the picturesque half-timbered houses, and following the river down the western side of the old city, the only place of interest is the **Église St-Pierre-le-Vieux** which consists of two churches, one Catholic and the other Protestant, and contains scenes of the Passion attributed to the late sixteenth-century painter Henri Lutzelmann who was a native of Strasbourg. From here the Rue du 22nd November makes a B-line for the **Place Kléber**, named after one of the city's most illustrious citizens. His statue in the centre, standing on a plinth recalling some of his more celebrated victories, was erected in 1840, nearly half a century after he was assassinated in Cairo. The Rue des Grandes Arcades links the Place Kléber with the Place Gutenberg, overlooked by the Hôtel du Com-

River boats are used for trips along the canals, Strasbourg

Street sellers in Strasbourg appear wherever there are tourists

The Barrage Vauban, Strasbourg

merce and only two short blocks from the cathedral, while the elderly but frequently restored **Église St-Pierre-le-Jeune** is slightly closer but in the opposite direction.

If the Place Kléber is the best-known square in Strasbourg, the Place Broglie certainly runs it a close second. This is not so much a square as a tree-filled avenue, dominated by the splendid Hôtel de Ville that was once the home of the counts of Hanau-Lichtenberg. It vies for attention with several other rather grand buildings of comparable age, the municipal theatre with its sculptured muses and columns and the monument to Maréchal Leclerc who liberated Strasbourg from the Germans in November 1944. The streets all round are full of elderly, eye-catching mansions and it is worth making a circular tour along the Rue Brulée, the Rue de l'Arc-en-Ciel, the Rue Pucelles, the Rue des Juifs and the Rue du Dôme in order to see them before crossing over the Canal des Faux-Remparts. This can be done by car or on foot using one of the footbridges that lead to the Avenue de la Marseillaise.

Once across the canal it would be almost impossible to miss the **Place de la République**, a large leafy complex containing a war memorial surrounded by an extensive circular garden, the ancient royal Palais du Rhin, the Théâtre National and the Bibliotheque Nationale. The Avenue de la Marseillaise runs down from the south-eastern corner of the Place de la République, crosses the River Ill and, changing its name to the Boulevard de la Victoire, leads to the Centre Universitaire with its fountains and gardens and an informative **Musée Zoologique de l'Université**. On the other hand the Contades, to the north of the Place de la République, contains the Synagogue de la Paix, built in 1955 to replace the original one that was destroyed in 1940. Other places of interest in the vicinity include the Orangerie, designed by Le Nôtre and altered to a certain extent for a visit by the Empress Joséphine after her coronation in 1804. The pavilion that was named after her had to be rebuilt following a fire in 1968 and is now used for temporary exhibitions, drama productions and concerts. The delightful old Alsatian farmhouse on the lake is occupied by one of the city's leading restaurants, the Buerehiesel. Its nearest neighbours are the **Palais de l'Europe**, opened in 1977 and occupied by the Council of Europe and the European Parliament, and beyond it, the Maison de la Radio-Télévision (Radio and Television Centre).

Strasbourg is the largest river port in France apart from Paris and a great deal of the area to the south and east is taken up by canals and basins fringed with installations, warehouses and all the other accoutrements required by a bustling maritime and commercial centre. Visitors whose interests lie in this direction can drive round without too much trouble by keeping to the main roads. One circular route from south of the Orangerie might well be down the Avenue de la Forêt-Noire to the Port d'Anvers, then south by way of the Route du Petit Rhin to join the N4, across the Bassin Vauban and along the Route du Rhin. Once across the next bridge the Rue Brigade Alsace-Lorrain cuts through the Place d'Austerlitz and, as the Rue d'Austerlitz, heads for the Pont du Corbeau, after which it is a more or less straight run through the old city to the Place Kléber. This is not nearly as complicated as it sounds but of course it is far easier to do the whole thing by boat, which takes about 3 hours. Alternatively, a trip on a pleasure steamer round the city and a few of its suburbs only lasts for roughly 1½ hours.

Because the River Rhine is the border between France and Germany there is literally nowhere to go in the Bas-Rhin east of Strasbourg, but the number of attractions to be found in every other direction more than make up for this. The best way to see as much as possible is to divide the region up into sections, using the capital as a starting point. Some people prefer to return to their hotel after every excursion, while others would rather make a comprehensive tour of the whole region, spending each night at a different town along the way. This means covering some sections of the route twice or else selecting the major places of interest and ignoring the rest.

Heading north from Strasbourg, the circular Route des Villages Pittoresque covers a total of about 160km (100 miles) although it can be adapted at any stage in order to turn back or travel further afield. Initially there are several alternative ways out of the city. Apart from the A4 *autoroute* there is the D468 to La Wantzenau, known principally for its restaurants, or the D263 to Brumath which has little of interest for the average tourist. However it provides the easiest and quickest route to **Haguenau**, an eleventh-century town founded by a member of the Hohenzollern family in the heart of an extensive forest.

Haguenau was a favourite retreat of the latter-day Holy Roman emperors and enjoyed a considerable measure of wealth and influence until it was destroyed in a series of battles culminating in the Thirty Years War. Somewhat bloody but nevertheless unbowed, the town pulled itself together and started restoring as much as possible before replacing everything else. One reminder of its days as a free, imperial city is the twelfth-century Église St-Georges, on the street of the same name, which still has its original bells. From here the Grand Rue becomes a pedestrian precinct through the heart of the old city and then continues in a slightly roundabout way to the Église St-Nicolas, which owes its existence to the Emperor Frédéric

The eleventh-century town of Haguenau

Antiquated houses in the Le Bruch quarter of Wissembourg

Barberousse. This 800-year-old church was severely damaged in 1940 but succeeded in preserving or restoring some of its ancient stonework. However, the splendid wooden panelling and the choir stalls originally belonged to the Abbaye de Neubourg and were only acquired at the time of the Revolution. The four wooden statues representing St-Augustin, St-Ambroise, St-Grégoire and St-Jérôme are known collectively as Les Pères de l'Église.

Apart from one or two elderly towers and a handful of eighteenth-century houses, there is a much-restored old building on the Rue de la Moder which has been adapted to house the Musée Alsacien. This shows an interest in every aspect of life in the province, whether it involves traditional costumes or cooking utensils, pottery, furniture, religion or local crafts. By way of contrast the Musée Historique, on the Rue Maréchal Foch, has much wider horizons, stretching from prehistoric times to the present day with exhibits that are interesting without being particularly memorable. Haguenau is also a good place for holidaymakers who prefer the outdoor life. It has one or two small hotels and facilities for swimming, riding, hunting and fishing in addition to long walks through the forest.

Anyone in search of pottery to take home would be well advised to visit **Soufflenheim**, 14km (9 miles) eastwards on the N63. In addition to its long-established pottery industry, some very modest Celtic and Roman excavations give weight to the theory that it is the site of a very old settlement. Alternatively, **Sessenheim**, a few kilometres to the south along the D737, owes its popularity to the fact that this charming little village was where Goethe conducted his love affair with Frédérique while he was a student at Strasbourg University. There is a small museum in the elderly Auberge au Boeuf which helps to keep the romance alive, assisted by the local church where her parents are buried and the nearby memorial to the poet which was erected in 1962.

The minor D344 from Soufflenheim wanders gently through the forest to **Betschdorf**, another typically attractive Alsatian village steeped in pottery making. Here some of the studios are open to visitors, exhibitions are held and a small museum makes a feature of the more unusual local designs. There are two alternative routes connecting Betschdorf with the D263, one of which crosses the road to call at Surbourg which has a small Romanesque church that was once attached to a Benedictine Abbey. Meanwhile the D263 presses on to **Hunspach** with its beautifully maintained half-timbered houses and authentic Alsatian costumes. Naturally these are only worn on special occasions, at other times the villagers dress in exactly the same way as everybody else.

The nearest place of any size to Hunspach is **Wissembourg** on the River Lauter, hard by the German border. It is a pleasantly atmospheric old town, full of very viewable antiquated houses, especially in the quarter known as Le Bruch. This is partly enclosed in ramparts and surrounded by water but is, nevertheless, within striking distance of the Église St-Pierre-et-St-Paul, a splendid Gothic pile that runs Strasbourg cathedral a fairly close second. It was built in the thirteenth century as an addition to a much older monastery which has now unfortunately disappeared. The church suffered a great deal at the hands of the Revolutionaries who were so enamoured with the guillotine that they decapitated the statues and destroyed much of the interior decoration before using it to store fodder for their horses. Despite all this there is still a trace of the original frescoes as well as a red sandstone tomb that has definitely seen better days and some early stained glass windows. Another survivor is the restored eleventh-century chapel in the ancient crypt.

The Avenue de la Sous-Préfecture runs down from the front of an elderly mansion, past the church and what little remains of the abbey, and nods at the Maison du Sel overlooking the water and the Hôtel de Ville standing almost opposite. Thereafter it changes its name to the Rue Nationale in order to reach the Holztapfel which was a busy coaching inn for more than 60 years. The house has a slight air of smug respectability, possibly because Napoléon stayed there in 1806, the year that he defeated Prussia and was riding high before the Russian winter of 1812 cut him down to size. Half a dozen little streets connect the Rue Nationale with the Promenade des Remparts where most of the defensive walls have been replaced by trees. Backing on to it is the Musée Westercamp which fills its sixteenth-century rooms with prehistoric odds and ends, items discarded by the Romans, some very worthwhile furniture, local costumes and reminders of the Battle of Wissembourg in 1870 that resulted in a Prussian victory. The town tends to become unusually crowded at Whitsun which marks the beginning of a special fair during which interest centres on processions, music and dancing, folklore, horses and traditional costumes.

The D3 from Wissembourg, via the Col du Pigeonnier with its views across the Alsatian plain to the Black Forest, is known as the Route des Châteaux Forts. It is clearly marked with signposts, giving motorists an opportunity to visit at least ten different fortified castles, some of which are nothing more than weatherbeaten ruins in an advanced state of decomposition. It is possible to inspect each and every one of them by simply parking the car, making sure that it is locked and that nothing has been left on the seats, and clambering up

a winding path through the trees that may or may not need some
professional attention. Sometimes this is hardly worth the effort, but
there are a few which are certainly worth seeing and others that have
at least something to recommend them. The Château de
Hohenbourg, for example, boasts the remains of a keep and some ill-
assorted statues while the nearby **Château de Fleckenstein** is both
closer to the D3 and a good deal more rewarding. It is a rather
splendid castle, built on a rock and reached along a minor turnoff a
few kilometres north of Lembach. Restoration work has been going
on for some time with the result that it even has a small museum.
Meanwhile, anyone who is more interested in modern warfare can
deviate slightly to join a guided tour of L'Ouvrage du Four à Chaux,
built as part of the Maginot Line about 1km (½ mile) south of the
village.

Back on the D3, **Niedersteinbach**, 8km (5 miles) from Lembach,
has a pleasant hotel with a tennis court and swimming pool, making
it a popular centre for hiking through the Parc Naturel Régional des
Vosges du Nord. Alternatively, the Anthon ☎ 88 09 55 01 in
Obersteinbach just down the road, is a popular restaurant with a
few rooms set aside for guests. It is just as convenient for people who
want to explore all the local strongholds by following a comprehensive network of paths marked out by the Club Vosgien through the
hilly, largely red sandstone countryside. On the other hand, motorists who would rather ride than ramble would probably be happier
in **Niederbronn-les-Bains**, which is only 34km (21 miles) from
Wissembourg. It is a thriving spa whose thermal springs were much
appreciated by the Romans in the first century AD, especially those
suffering from arthritis or rheumatism. The town fell on hard times
during the Dark Ages but was restored by Count Philippe de Hanau
in the sixteenth century, after which it went from strength to
strength. These days it has a variety of baths to choose from, the
comfortable Grand Hotel on the Avenue Foch, ☎ 88 09 02 60, several
smaller establishments, some good restaurants, a casino, tennis
courts and parks laid out with trees and flowers.

Within easy reach of Niederbronn-les-Bains, only a short drive but
a longish walk to the north, are the ruins of two thirteenth-century
castles known as Old Windstein and New Windstein. Their attendant village has bicycles for hire and guides are available for parties
of seven or more people who want to explore the surrounding area
using some 30 or 40km (20 or 25 miles) of country lanes and cycle
tracks. Whichever way you turn in this part of the country you are
almost certain to stub your toe on the remnants of a dilapidated
fortress. The **Château de Falkenstein** is a prime example, largely on

account of its caves which are partly natural and partly manmade and include the vast Salle des Gardes. Among its other attractions are a resident ghost who is said to get a bit restless at midnight, and a splendid view from the top. Away to the north-west is the rather woebegone Château de Waldeck standing guard over the Étang de Hanau, a pleasing expanse of water where swimming and boating are encouraged but fishing is forbidden.

From Niederbronn-les-Bains the Route des Villages Pittoresque calls at Reichshoffen on its way to **Woerth**, 10km (6 miles) to the east. This village was one of the local hot spots during the Franco-Prussian War and relives its past with the help of some 4,000 tin soldiers drawn up for battle in the Musée du 6 Août 1870. Also on display is all the paraphernalia of war dating from around 1870. The D27 links Woerth with Haguenau on the way back to Strasbourg while any number of little roads strike out westwards across an area peppered with small hamlets in the general direction of **La Petite-Pierre**.

One good reason for stopping in this delightful hilltop village is that it has a selection of most acceptable hotels, two of them with tennis courts and indoor swimming pools. Aux Trois Roses, an eighteenth-century *auberge* on the main street, ☎ 88 70 45 02, is both charming and informal with a garden, parking space and a play area for children. It can provide suites as well as double and single rooms but those on the front can be rather noisy. Some 800 or 900 years ago La Petite Pierre consisted of little more than a fortified château, but this was rebuilt towards the end of the sixteenth century and later the small community was protected by ramparts designed by Vauban. Some of these are still standing and incorporate an old storehouse known as the Magazin which fancies itself as a popular art museum. The Chapelle St-Louis, built in 1684, has its own Musée du Sceau Alsacien dealing with various aspects of local history. The village is well placed for outdoor enthusiasts, so much so that short all-in walking or cycling holidays can be arranged through the Association pour le Développement des Vosges du Nord in the Maison du Parc.

One or two villages in the surrounding area have something quite unexpected to offer. A case in point is **Graufthal**, on the D122, which can be reached just as easily by hikers using either the GR53 or the GR532. It was partly inhabited by troglodytes until about 30 years ago and some of their old cave dwellings can still be seen, hollowed out of the red sandstone.

Neuwiller-lès-Saverne, somewhat further away to the east, is known principally for the Église St-Pierre-et-St-Paul which was updated in the ninth century in order to provide a tomb for St Adelphe. There is a fair amount to see both inside and outside but

The twelfth-century château at Haute-Barr known as the Œil de l'Alsace commands a view of the plain

Le Metzig in Molsheim, vaguely similar to the Maison des Têtes in Colmar

pride of place goes to the two superimposed chapels that were added about 200 years later. One of them contains some fine tapestries recalling the life and miraculous works of the saint. **St-Jean-Saverne**, a few kilometres to the south and bypassed by the A4 *autoroute*, also has an elderly church and some tapestries but is more usually associated with flowers and witchcraft. The Chapelle St-Michel, some 2km (1 mile) from the town, shares its vantage point with a circle in the rock called L'Ecole des Sorcières, where witches are said to gather at night to exchange notes and concoct their magic brews. At sunrise they all retire to the Trou des Sorcières, a grotto at the bottom of a long flight of steps and originally intended as a tomb, where they are sure of being undisturbed, except by sightseers on Sunday afternoons.

Saverne itself is infinitely larger with a whole variety of attractions that are much more tangible. Its most impressive building is undoubtedly the vast eighteenth-century château which has a majestic façade, Corinthian columns, wide sweeping steps and extensive gardens bounded by the Canal de la Marne au Rhin. Part of it is given over to a museum that dabbles in archaeology, local history, religious sculptures and mementoes of the Rohan family who were the Prince-Bishops of Strasbourg. However many of Saverne's most illustrious visitors, among them a brace of kings and Louis de Rohan, the cardinal who blotted his copybook over the affair of Marie-Antoinette's necklace, had their apartments in the older château down the road. It is just on the other side of the Église Paroissiale which first saw the light of day about 900 years ago but has been restored and updated considerably since then. Inside are the tombs of two bishops, an assortment of statues and wood carving and some medieval stained glass windows, while anything connected with the Gauls, the Romans and the Franks has been relegated to the gardens outside.

On the other side of the Grand Rue are a pair of rather nice old houses and, beyond them, the Ancien Cloître des Récollets, built in 1303 as part of the local convent, with a collection of murals that were added a good deal later. On the far side of the canal, adjoining the Route de Paris, is a large Roseraie containing some 1,300 different varieties of roses. Roughly 3km (2 miles) further on are the Jardin Botanique du Col de Saverne and the Saut de Prince-Charles. The garden has well over 2,000 different kinds of plants and adjoins the cliff which, according to legend, a certain Prince Charles and his horse negotiated at a single leap. For lesser mortals there is a path down to the bottom and a grotto that was created for some obscure reason in 1524. Another attraction on the outskirts of Saverne is the ruined Château de Haut-Barr. It dates back to the twelfth century and is known as the Œil de l'Alsace (Eye of Alsace) on account of the view, which stretches as far as the spire of Strasbourg cathedral.

Marmoutier, south of Saverne on the N4, owes its existence to St-Léobard, a disciple of St-Colomban who arrived from Ireland in the sixth century, tried to show the rulers of Burgundy the error of their ways and, as a result, had to move swiftly on into Italy out of harm's way. Meanwhile St-Léobard founded a monastery which adopted the name of its Abbé Maur 200 years later and, as Marmoutier, continued to function until it was overtaken by the Revolution. The large, rather grim and forbidding church of St-Stephen has a Roman façade, a thirteenth-century nave, some quite attractive choir stalls and an eighteenth-century organ. As there is nothing else to see, a good idea is to press on down the N4 to **Avolsheim**. Here the main attractions are the Dompeter, a primitive Romanesque church with stout walls and squat pillars that was consecrated by Pope Léon in 1094, some mural paintings in a baptistry of comparable age and a linden tree outside the church where it is believed to have been growing for the last 1,000 years.

Molsheim, just a trifle further on, is larger and busier, being one of the most northerly towns on the famous Route du Vin. This starts at Marlenheim and threads its way through vineyards and atmospheric little wine centres to Cernay, in the Haut-Rhin, between Thann and Mulhouse. Molsheim is an attractive little place of about the same vintage as Avolsheim's linden tree and takes its position as a tourist centre very seriously. The Hotel Diana, near the Pont de la Bruche, ☎ 88 38 51 59, is both convenient and comfortable and is not far from the traditional home of the famous Bugatti cars. However, the most eye-catching building is Le Metzig, or Slaughter House, built by the Corps des Bouchers in the Place de l'Hôtel de Ville in 1554. It would be difficult to find anything that looks less like an abattoir. There are twin stairways leading up to a large reception room on the first floor, balconies resplendent with windowboxes filled with flowers, decorative stonework reminiscent of the Maison des Têtes in Colmar and double doors leading to a small museum. In addition there is a vault where visitors are invited to sample the local wines. Only a block away, down the Rue Strasbourg, the old Porte de Ville was originally part of the fortifications. Quite close by, almost within striking distance of the Pont de la Bruche, is a church that belonged to the Académie des Jésuites, founded by Archduke Leopold in 1618. It makes quite interesting viewing, having been expertly restored a little over 20 years ago. Molsheim is also a popular centre for swimming, riding, fishing and shooting as well as

One of the old gates into the village of Rosheim

Most of Obernai's main attractions are grouped around the Place du Marché

for walking and taking short sightseeing trips.

If no accommodation is available in Molsheim, which could well be the case during the Wine Fair at the beginning of May, the Hotel Parc on the Rue du Général-Gouraud, ☎ 88 95 50 08, in **Obernai** would be a good alternative. The towns are only 10km (6 miles) apart and Obernai, besides being more picturesque, has the advantage of a close association with Ste-Odile, the patron saint of Alsace. After a long and turbulent history, starting with a twelfth-century abbey, followed by the addition of fortifications that withstood attacks by the Armagnacs and the Burgundians, it was devastated during the Thirty Years War and finally annexed by Louis XIV in 1679. Apart from the Église St-Pierre-et-St-Paul, reconstructed out of all recogni- tion in the nineteenth century, most of the main attractions are grouped around the Place du Marché in the centre of the old town. They include the Hôtel de Ville and the Tour de la Chapelle, which is actually a thirteenth-century belfry, the Halle aux Blés and the Puits aux Six-Seaux, an extrovert Renaissance well with a canopy supported on decorative columns and six buckets planted with flowers. Both the fountain in the Place du Marché and the statue of Ste-Odile were added nearly a hundred years ago.

Visitors and pilgrims gather for a service in the chapel at Mont-Ste-Odile

There are one or two small places of interest within a few kilometres of Obernai. **Rosheim**, to the north-west, shelters behind the remains of its original ramparts, pointing its visitors in the direction of the typically Romanesque church of St-Pierre-et-St-Paul and an assortment of antiquated houses lining the narrow streets leading off the Rue du Général-de-Gaulle. Among its other attractions are the sombre Maison Romane, built in the twelfth century, and the Porte Basse, one of three fortified gateways added during the Middle Ages.

Motorists with a day or so to spare will find plenty of variety in the area to the west of Obernai known as the Région du Hohwald. One of the best circular tours starts out from Ottrott to Klingenthal and then changes to the D204 in order to inspect the remains of the fortified **Château de Guirbaden** which consists of a keep, a twelfth-century chapel and a few doors and walls. Thereafter the road bypasses the Signal de Grendelbruch, known for its splendid panoramic views, and carries on to Schirmeck which floodlights its castle and organises walking tours through the mountains.

From here the N420 proceeds in a leisurely fashion to Rothau, a modest hamlet barely 11km (7 miles) from **Colroy-la-Roche**, down the road apiece and along the secondary D424. The main, if not the only, reason for driving on to Colroy-la-Roche is to book in at the Hostellerie la Cheneaudiere, ☎ 88 97 61 64. It is a comfortable, modern establishment with some ground floor rooms, providing excellent food in addition to a tennis court, a sauna and a heated indoor swimming pool. Guests can work off any surplus energy riding, walking in the forest, hunting or fishing for trout in one of the little mountain streams. During the winter months there is some modest skiing about 5km (3 miles) away.

Visitors who are only out for the day should ignore Colroy-la-Roche altogether and, instead, make a sharp lefthand turn at Rothau on to the D130 in order to complete the original circuit. Some 8km (5 miles) from Rothau, **Le Struthof** is the site of a former Nazi concentration camp where hundreds of people were held until they either died or were deported to other camps in Germany. It is a predictably depressing place with its barbed wire, dingy cells and large memorial.

At the point where the D130 joins the D426 two options are open to motorists, both of them considerably more inviting. To the north is **Mont-Ste-Odile**, the site of a convent founded by the saint which is still an important place of pilgrimage. It marks one end of the strange Pagan Wall, built of enormous limestone blocks between about 1000 and 800BC that wanders around the plateau for several kilometres in an indecisive manner without giving any obvious reason for its existence. The little Chapelle Ste-Odile, said to have been built over the cell where she died, is the only part of the original convent to have escaped a disastrous fire in 1546. It contains some unspecified relics of the saint and is linked to the Chapelle de la Croix where her father is buried. Among other things to be seen are a seventeenth-century church, the Chapelle des Larmes and the Chapelle des Anges, neither of whose mosaics are more than 50 or 60 years old, and the nearby Fontaine de Ste-Odile. This is a little spring, protected by a grille, which is associated with one of the miracles of Ste-Odile and is said to work wonders for believers who have trouble with their eyes.

From Mont Ste-Odile it is only a few kilometres back to Ottrott and Obernai. However, by following the D426 in the opposite direction it is possible to find a comfortable hotel at **Le Hohwald**, a mountain resort in the heart of a large plantation consisting mainly of fir trees. A choice of twisting minor roads connects it with Champ du Fer, one of the high spots of the area with an observation tower that looks out in all directions, over the cornfields of the Bruche Valley, across into Germany and southwards on a clear day to the Alpes Bernoises. Although it cannot compare with any of the famous Alpine resorts it is, nevertheless, a modest winter sports centre, rather short on hotels but providing both chalets and mountain huts.

Back on the Route du Vin the hillsides are blanketed in vines tended by small rural communities and littered with the remains of ancient châteaux. One typical village is **Andlau** which grew up round a Benedictine abbey founded by Ste-Richarde, the wife of Emperor Charles le Gros, towards the end of the ninth century. After her husband had accused her of being unfaithful, and she had gone to considerable lengths to prove her innocence, she escaped into the forest where an angel appeared and told her to build a convent. When it was finished she moved in and before long it was recognised as a haven for other wives in similar circumstances. The convent continued to flourish for the next 800 years but then went into a decline and eventually disappeared during the Revolution. However, the extremely decorative Église Ste-Richarde, built soon after she was canonised in 1049, is in an excellent state of repair. It has an impressive porch, attractive stalls, the shrine of the saint and a rather splendid original crypt.

Another village worth seeing on the Route du Vin is **Dambach-la-Ville**. It is a photogenic little place with three ancient gateways, the remnants of its old fortifications, plenty of elderly houses and a profusion of flowers. The Chapelle St-Sébastien, on the outskirts, claims to have the richest Baroque altar in Alsace and is certainly more appealing than the fifteenth-century charnel-house. It is a longish walk from the chapel to the ruined twelfth-century Château

de Bernstein which, considering the number of weatherbeaten fortresses with reasonable views just waiting to be visited, turns out to
be fairly run-of-the-mill.

Sélestat, reached along any of the minor roads that connect with
the more important routes into the town, consists of an ancient heart
surrounded by modern industrial suburbs. It has some excellent
restaurants but remarkably few hotels, although there is a holiday
village in the vicinity, so it is advisable to drive the 9km (6 miles) to
St-Hippolyte and book in at the Hotel Munsch (☎ 89 73 00 09), also
known as Aux Ducs de Lorraine. It is a pleasing mansion on the
Route du Vin adjoining the owner's vineyards but it may be rather
crowded in August, especially while Sélestat holds its traditional
procession of flowers combined with a wine festival on the second
Sunday of the month.

Many people equate Sélestat with its famous Bibliothèque
Humaniste (Humanist Library), founded in 1452. It is housed in the
ancient Halle aux Blés on the Place Gambetta and contains a great
many rare books and manuscripts, some of them dating from the
seventh century. Also on display are items usually found in a
museum such as prehistoric exhibits, wooden sculptures, an early
funeral mask, jewellery and pottery. A stone's throw away down the
Rue de l'Église, beyond the Porte Renaissance which belongs to the
Hôtel des Bénédictins d'Ebersmunster, the Gothic Église St-Georges
was extensively restored in the nineteenth century. Its most interesting features are the windows whose subjects range from heavenly
musicians to episodes from the lives of Ste-Catherine and Ste-Agnès.
The Église Ste-Foy, down the Rue du Babil, is fractionally older,
having been built in the twelfth century on the remains of an even
older church. In the crypt below the triple nave are traces of the
round church of St-Sépulcre which was part of an ancient Benedictine priory.

A few blocks away, beyond the Place d'Armes, are three more old
buildings — the Église des Récollets in the Place du Marché-aux-
Pots, the Maison de Stephan Ziegler, built in the sixteenth century,
on the Rue de Verdun, and the Ancien Arsenal Ste-Barbe, much
beloved by local storks. The walls and towers which had defended
the old town throughout the Middle Ages were pulled down in the
seventeenth century on the orders of Louis XIV. However, two
isolated pieces were left standing — the Tour des Sorcières overlooking the Place Porte de Strasbourg, behind the Église St-Georges, and
the Tour de l'Horloge at the southern end of the Rue des Chevaliers.
The rest was partly replaced with new fortifications designed by
Vauban, but a large percentage of these has also disappeared. A short

section is still in existence along the Boulevard Vauban, known as the Promenade des Remparts and, apart from anything else, it has a commanding view across country to the vast medieval fortress of Haut-Koenigsbourg.

Roughly mid-way between Sélestat and Haut-Koenigsbourg the village of **Kintzheim** claims to have one of the best preserved Gothic castles in Alsace. It is, of course, a ruin like so many others of its ilk but it is worth seeing for a number of reasons, among them the little chapel and the knights' banqueting hall which some people say is haunted. Two other very different local attractions are the Parcs d'Animaux de Kintzheim, the first of them concentrating mainly on monkeys while the second is only interested in birds of prey. The Volerie des Aigles has several different types apart from eagles, such as falcons, condors and vultures, and some of them are trained to take part in special displays in the castle courtyard, but only if the weather is good. Meanwhile the Montagne des Singes is reserved for monkeys that can adapt to life outdoors in Alsace.

Kintzheim, like Haut-Koenigsbourg, is on the invisible line that separates Bas-Rhin from Haut-Rhin and anyone staying nearby at St-Hippolyte has already crossed over it and is well on the way to Colmar, 20km (12 miles) to the south.

HAUT-RHIN

Colmar, the main town in the Haut-Rhin, is not only an exceptionally lovely centre but it also has a comfortable, if rather run-of-the-mill hotel near the station, a selection of quite adequate establishments and a handful of excellent restaurants close to hand. Other, similar hotels and restaurants are situated on the outskirts in addition to a motel on the road to Strasbourg which unfortunately does not have a restaurant at the moment.

Among the town's earliest admirers was Charlemagne who stayed there on several occasions with his son, Louis le Débonnaire. It blossomed in the Middle Ages, due mainly to the wine trade and, although it suffered in successive wars, not least of them World War I and World War II, it has managed to preserve a sizeable collection of ancient buildings and a very delightful atmosphere.

The old quarter is conveniently small, having most of its outstanding attractions clustered round the Place de l'Ancienne-Douane and the Place de la Cathédrale, with the remainder only a gentle stroll away. One of these is the Musée d'Unterlinden, at the far end of the Rue des Clefs, which claims to be the most frequently-visited museum of any in France apart from those in Paris. The building started life as a Dominican convent and still has its thirteenth-century arcaded cloister and the original chapel housing Mathias Grünewald's famous Issenheim Altarpiece. This includes a rather unusual version of the Crucifixion which is most effective, as well as a surprisingly sparsely-attended *mise au tombeau*. Among other things to look for in the chapel are paintings by local artists of the same period and the statues of St-Antoine, St-Jérôme and St-Augustin, thought to be the work of Nicolas de Haguenau. The first floor of the building is devoted to museum pieces such as costumes, weapons, porcelain and other items connected with the history of Alsace. Additional galleries are set aside for anything from prehistory to Gallo-Roman remains and early paintings by unknown artists to modern works by men of the calibre of Léger and Picasso.

A mere stone's throw away is a decorative Renaissance mansion known as the Maison des Têtes, roughly half way down the street that has been called after it. The house gets its name from a number of sculptured heads that share the façade with ornamental windows, iron and stone work and an elaborate doorway leading to a restaurant designed to blend in with the surroundings. On the far side of the same block the Église des Dominicians owes its existence to the Emperor Rodolphe de Habsbourg, although it was not completed in its present form until the fifteenth century. The church's prize possession is Martin Schongauer's *La Vierge au Buisson de Roses*, depicting the Virgin dressed in scarlet, seated in a rose bower and holding an attractive Child, surrounded by flowers and little blue birds and attended by angels. The slightly larger Église St-Martin on the Place de la Cathédrale is only a short walk down the Rue des Serruriers and dates from roughly the same era. It makes no attempt to surpass its neighbour's statue of King Solomon, preferring instead to rely for attention on its original stained glass windows and some interesting statues in the side chapels.

Opposite this collegiate church the Rue des Marchands breaks out in a rash of historic buildings. The nearest is the ancient Corps de Garde, built in 1575, where the local magistrates once sat in judgement, while half-hidden behind it is the Maison Adolphe dating from 1350 and reputed to be the oldest house in Colmar. The Maison Pfister, just next door, is liberally decorated with frescoes and medallions and overlooks both the little Maison au Cygne, on the opposite side of the road, and the birthplace of the sculptor Frédéric Auguste Bartholdi who died in 1904. Part of this building has been turned into a museum and contains, among other exhibits, items which once belonged to the man whose works include the memorial to Martin Schongauer and the *Lion of Belfort*. However he is undoubtedly most widely known for his *Statue of Liberty* in New York harbour.

There are just as many eye-catching old buildings strung out along the Grand Rue, a block or so away. They range from the former Customs House to the Maison des Arcades, standing cheek by jowl with the ancient Franciscan church of St-Matthieu, visited mainly for its fifteenth-century crucifixion and stained glass windows. Behind the Schwendi fountain, one of several other examples of the work of Bartholdi, the old Tanners' Quarter has been meticulously restored, in keeping with the Ancien Hôpital, built on very generous lines in the Classical style. From here it is a pleasant and undemanding walk to the Pont St-Pièrre over the Lauch with its much-photographed view of La Petite Venise. This is an enchanting spot where elderly houses overhang the still waters of the canal, framed by trees, festooned with flowers and disturbed by nothing more aggravating than an occasional punt or rowing boat.

Colmar takes its responsibilities as a popular tourist centre very seriously. It lays on conducted tours and longer excursions by coach during the season, when many of its most outstanding attractions are illuminated; whereas, for people who are only interested in sporting activities, it provides facilities for swimming and riding. In addition, as the centre of the wine industry, it holds an exuberant Foire aux Vines in mid-August, with the emphasis on folklore and wine tasting, followed quite swiftly by the Journées de la Choucroute that spills over into September.

For the enthusiastic sightseer there are any number of different places to see within a short distance of Colmar. To start in the east, **Neuf-Brisach**, only 16km (10 miles) distant along the N415, is an extremely atmospheric little citadel with an enormous square Place d'Armes right in the middle. The village itself is in the form of a perfect octagonal, held firmly in shape by a double line of massive defensive walls built by Vauban that did their duty manfully during the siege of 1870. It is possible to take a half-hour walk along part of the ramparts from the Porte de Colmar to the Porte de Belfort. The latter gives houseroom to a small museum dedicated to Vauban, the French soldier and engineer who was responsible for the defences of almost every fortress along the borders of France during the reign of Louis XIV. There are one or two modest hotels in the vicinity, which are usually fully booked for the Lily of the Valley festival on 1 May, as well as the Motel Européen on the Ile du Rhin (☎ 89 72 51 57) with an 18-hole golf course a few miles away. During the summer months boat trips are organised for holidaymakers while an elderly steam train operates between Neuf-Brisach and Marckolsheim, just over the border in the Bas-Rhin. Marckolsheim is mainly interested these days in the hydro-electric system but it once formed part of the Maginot Line and recalls the fact with a memorial and a museum devoted to the battles of the Rhine.

Some 5km (3 miles) east of Neuf-Brisach the Grand Canal d'Alsace keeps company with the Rhine. This vast waterway is a magnificent sight with its giant locks, hydro-electric plant and sleek bridges carrying the main road across on to the central island where there is plenty of space for camping. From here it makes its final leap over the Rhine to Breisach-am-Rhein in Germany. For motorists who want to explore the area still further the D52 follows the contours of the Grand Canal d'Alsace southwards to a point a few miles from the Swiss frontier.

North and north-east of Colmar the countryside is peppered with fascinating little towns and villages. The main route to the north —

The enchanting La Petite Venise near the Quartier des Tanneurs, Colmar

the N83 — bypasses both the airport and the Parc Naturel de
Schoppenwihr marginally beyond it. This pleasant area was designed well over a hundred years ago with its shady paths, rare trees,
a lake and an elderly château of no particular interest to tourists. Nor
is it really worth turning off the N83 to inspect Ostheim which was
destroyed during World War II and had to be entirely rebuilt along
with its railway station and a Martyrs' Wall that provides a home for
storks.

A little further up the main road the D106 branches off to the left
and heads for **Ribeauvillé**, a small town on the Route du Vin nestling
against the green foothills of the Vosges. It is particularly well known
for its traditional festivals, among them the Fête du Kougelhof in
early June, the Foire aux Vines towards the end of July and the time-
honoured Fiddlers' Day on the first Sunday in September, when the
emphasis is on history. This is also the occasion on which bystanders
are invited to help themselves from the Fontaine de Vin in front of the
town hall, an invitation which is very seldom ignored. As an added
attraction the Hôtel de Ville has set aside enough space for a modest
local museum (afternoon guided tours when the Hôtel de Ville is
open).

A number of the picturesque old buildings in Ribeauvillé date
back to the sixteenth century, especially those in the vicinity of the
Tour des Bouchers, part of which is older by three centuries although
it collected most of its decorations in 1536. In addition to a Renaissance fountain and the fifteenth-century parish church of St-
Grégoire-le-Grand, the town has no less than three ruined castles to
its credit, all within reasonable climbing distance. Château de
Guisberg, abandoned for the past 400 years, still has its keep and the
remains of a round tower while the Château du Haut Ribeaupierre
contents itself with a round keep and a superb view. However, the
Château de St-Ulrich, clearly visible from the Grand Rue, is undoubtedly the most rewarding. It was once the home of the Comtes de
Ribeaupierre and inside the battered remnants of its outer fortifications has managed to preserve part of the château itself, including a
number of decorated windows carved with *fleurs de lys*. Anyone who
plans to spend a few days exploring the surrounding area would be
well advised to book in at the elegant Clos Saint-Vincent on the road
to Bergheim, which is a very up-market restaurant with a few
comfortable rooms for guests, ☎ 89 73 67 65.

Bergheim, almost on the doorstep, has its own defensive walls
and towers, a fourteenth-century Gothic church (enquire at the
presbytery, Rue de L'Église if closed) and a linden tree, said to be
1,000 years old. The village is often visited by German tourists on

their way to a nearby cemetery where members of their countrymen who were killed in World War II are buried. Alternatively, to the west of Ribeauvillé, the scenic D416 beyond the Château de St-Ulrich, makes its convoluted way through the mountains to **Ste-Marie-aux-Mines**, a distance of about 19km (12 miles). This was once a busy mining area, producing both silver and lead. Nowadays, during the summer months, the silver workings at St-Barthelemy are open to visitors. St-Pierre-sur-l'Hâte, built in the fifteenth century, was the original miners' church, in addition to which the Musée Minéralogique is full of appropriate items, augmented by a special exhibition at the beginning of July.

Motorists with only a passing interest in mining would probably opt instead for a pleasant secondary road that runs due north from Bergheim to St-Hippolyte, a charming little place surrounded by vineyards in the shadow of **Château du Haut-Koenigsbourg**. This massive fortress that has dominated the surrounding area for more than 800 years, was burned down by Swedish forces in the seventeenth century, thereby earning for itself the title of the most superb ruin in Alsace. Rebuilding work was started on the orders of Kaiser Wilhelm II about 100 years ago and, although there is still a certain amount to be done, a large section of the castle has been opened to visitors. Among its main attractions are private apartments, some containing appropriate furniture, a chapel and the Hall of Knights. From the Grand Bastion, with panoramic views stretching from the Black Forest to the Grand Ballon, sentries could keep an eye on a handful of other castles in the area for signs of any suspicious activity.

Riquewihr, 4½km (3 miles) south of Ribeauvillé, is a perfect example of a small medieval town that has largely ignored the passage of time. It is thought to have started life as *Richovilla*, the domain of an early Roman patrician called *Richo*, but for some reason changed its name prior to 1094. In the early fourteenth century it was given the status of a city and became the property of the Ducs de Wurtemberg, although this did not prevent it from suffering all the trials and tribulations of the period. In 1753 the current Duc got into financial difficulties and had to borrow a large sum of money from Voltaire, guaranteeing the loan by pledging his vineyards at Riquewihr. Today they still produce the same high quality wines, particularly Riesling, which are exported to countries all over the world. The historic cellars belonging to several of the local winegrowers are open to visitors and are well worth seeing.

Probably Riquewihr's best-known landmark is the Dolder, an extremely decorative fortified gatehouse built as part of the defences in 1291, updated and refurbished on two subsequent occasions and currently occupied by the Musée de la Société d'Archéologie. The museum covers a wide range of interests from everyday articles and furniture to the history of the area in peace and war. At the opposite end of the town the château of the Wurtembergs, dating from 1539, is home to the Musée d'Histoire des P.T.T. d'Alsace. This traces the history of the local communications systems from Gallo-Roman times to the present day — contrasting letters carried by messengers on foot or on horse-back, through the advent of stage coaches and the railways, to the introduction of airmail, telegrams and telephones. The exhibits include documents and photographs, stamps and early postcards along with a wealth of other paraphernalia. For collectors it also offers a special philatelist's bureau.

The streets of Riquewihr are lined with extremely picturesque old houses, many of whose wooden balconies are all but smothered in brightly coloured flowers. Among the most eye-catching are the Maison Kiener on the Rue du Cerf, opposite a sixteenth-century tavern, the Maison Preiss-Zimmer and the Nid de Cigognes (Storks' Nest House) built slightly earlier in 1535, which has a most attractive courtyard and a large wine press that is nearly 200 years old. Most of the ramparts have disappeared, apart from a section overlooking the Cour des Bergers, the original town gate, complete with a portcullis and the Wurtemberg coat-of-arms, and the ancient Tour des Voleurs. This so-called Robbers Tower was once a prison incorporating a torture chamber that was kept busy for centuries dealing with political prisoners and common thieves but is now nothing more than a popular tourist attraction.

Within easy reach of the town there is a four-star campsite and several marked footpaths through extensive forests of pine and chestnuts. One of them runs due south to **Kientzheim** where it is worth pausing in order to visit the Musée du Vin d'Alsace. This has been established in the château of the Knights of St-Stephen and is full of equipment connected with the industry. The village has managed to retain some of its original fortifications including the Porte Basse and a selection of very viewable old houses. The church, with its much restored Gothic tower, contains some fourteenth-century frescoes, several statues of the Virgin and the tomb of Lazare de Schwendi who is thought to have introduced Tokay into Alsace from Hungary. On the other hand the Chapelle Sts-Félix et Régule is notable mainly for its collection of rather strange ex-voto offerings, which may be almost anything left by people in search of divine assistance or gifts in appreciation of past favours.

Kientzheim forms a triangle of sorts with **Ammerschwir**, due south, and Kaysersberg, slightly to the west. The former was badly damaged towards the end of World War II and had to be largely rebuilt. The Église St-Martin still has its Renaissance staircase and some original statues but the windows had to be replaced after the fighting ended. The Porte Haute, once part of the fortifications, relies for attention on its unusual sundial, flaunts the town's coat-of-arms and provides an ideal nesting place for storks.

From Ammerschwir it is only a very short drive along the N415 to **Kaysersberg** which is slightly larger and just as interested in wine as any of its neighbours. It also boasts a comfortable hotel, the Résidence Chambard in the Rue du Genéral de Gaulle, ☎ 89 47 10 17 which is in reality an excellent restaurant with rooms attached. One of the village's main claims to fame is that it was the birthplace of Albert Schweitzer, the famous doctor and musician who won his Nobel Prize in 1952. The house where he was born has, predictably, been turned into a museum. Within easy strolling distance there are one or two rather nice old houses, a ruined château reputed to have been built by the Emperor Frédéric II and a fortified bridge from the fifteenth century which is still in good working order. Beyond it the Musée Communal specialises in religious art, local souvenirs and a few reminders of the Romans who passed through on more than one occasion during their repeated forays up and down the Rhine. The Holy Cross church, further along the Rue du Général de Gaulle, started life in the twelfth century and is justly proud of its Roman-esque façade and the statue of the Emperor Constantine as well as all the paintings and statues inside. The Chapelle St-Michel, a compara-tive newcomer in 1463, makes its bid for attention with an ossuary, some decorative frescoes and an unusual crucifix.

There are any number of small villages tucked away in the surrounding area, all offering modest *auberges*, invigorating moun-tain walks and, generally speaking, a bus service as well. Orbey goes one better with a motel, a nice line in Munster cheese and excursions to the Lac Noir and the Lac Blanc, carved out by ancient glaciers. On the other hand, motorists who only walk when it is absolutely necessary, tend to ignore most of these out-of-the-way attractions and are satisfied with an overall view of the lakes on their way to join the Route des Crêtes at the Col du Calvaire, near the Forêt des deux Lacs.

Alternatively, as Kaysersberg is only 11km (7 miles) from Colmar, there should be plenty of time to deviate from the main road to visit **Turckheim**. It boasts three ancient gateways, decorates its fountain with flowers, employs a night watchman to add to the atmosphere during the season and has both buses and a railway station. The village is only a few minutes' drive from Colmar but somewhat further from Gunsbach where Albert Schweitzer lived for a while. His house has also been turned into a museum, filled with mementoes of the famous doctor that touch on several facets of his character, such as books and music, medicine, sermons and photographs. It is not very extensive and the guided tours only last for about half an hour.

Anyone planning a day trip south of Colmar has a variety of different options to choose from, depending on time and inclination. The quickest and least interesting of them is the A35 *autoroute* which ignores everything in its path and even skirts round Mulhouse on the way to Basel. However there is a get-out point through **Ensisheim** which was the seat of the regents of the Habsburg emperors in the fifteenth and sixteenth centuries. The Hôtel de Ville and the Hôtel de la Couronne are two of its most eye-catching buildings. The former contains a small Musée Historique which is included in a guided tour any weekday morning or afternoon, whereas the latter has been converted into a restaurant with a dozen or so rooms on the premises.

Slightly to the east, the village of **Ungersheim** is nothing much to write home about but it did provide more than 25 acres (10 hectares) of open country in 1980 for what has grown into the fascinating, open-air Écomusée de Haut-Alsace. This was created in the guise of a typical small community, the only difference being that it was designed to show every facet of rural life since the Middle Ages. Each house is different, having been removed from its original location and carefully reconstructed in the correct section with due regard to its age and individual features. For example, there is a fortified mansion from the twelfth century in the area devoted to Mulhouse. Schlierbach and Luemschwiller provide a farmhouse and barn that could well have belonged to a rich countryman in the Sundgau region at the time of the Peasants' Revolt 400 years later, while Ribeauvillé is represented by an eighteenth-century garden house in the form of a tower. Some of the buildings have been left unfinished in order to demonstrate exactly how they were constructed. A number of houses have been furnished to show precisely how the owners lived in the days when they were occupied. In addition, all the other aspects of village life are faithfully represented with such things as an oil mill, a carpenter's shop and a bakery whose wood fire oven turns out delicious bread. The village has its own pond, most of the usual farm animals and a special enclosure for storks. It also includes a small hotel, a restaurant built over a sixteenth-century cellar, a children's play area and conference rooms.

An alternative choice for motorists heading south from Colmar with sightseeing in mind would be to rejoin the Route du Vin at **Eguisheim**, which claims to have been the birthplace of Pope Leo IX but has nothing very convincing to substantiate this. Nevertheless, the modern windows in the church perpetuate the story with various scenes from his life. It is an attractive little village with a number of well-preserved half-timbered houses, world-weary ruins and a modest art gallery that also dabbles in archaeology. For anyone in search of even more relics from the past it is well-placed for an excursion round the Route des Cinq-Châteaux (Route of the Five Castles), covering a total distance of about 20km (12 miles).

Further south on the N83 **Rouffach** boasts a very up-market hotel, the expensive and beautifully converted Château d'Isenbourg, on a hill outside the town. It has a tennis court, a swimming pool which is heated and an ornamental lake floodlit, like the courtyard, in the evening. The tasteful decor and furnishings and an excellent restaurant in the fifteenth-century vaulted cellar all contribute to its pleasing atmosphere. The hotel has a few ground floor rooms suitable for disabled guests but it is as well to book in advance, especially in the spring and autumn when it holds musical weekends and soirées, ☎ 89 49 63 53.

The town of Rouffach compliments the château, weighing in with a decorative Renaissance town hall, a selection of old gabled houses and the Tour des Sorcières dating from the thirteenth century and providing a convenient home for storks. The Église Notre-Dame de l'Assomption, reputed to be the oldest Gothic building in Haut-Alsace, has a transept which is about 800 years old, although the façade was added some 200 years later. Southwards from Rouffach there are few places of interest before the N83 makes contact with the N66 beyond Cernay.

The industrial town of **Cernay** is sometimes described as a tourist centre although it has very little to interest the average visitor, give or take a small history museum in the Porte de Thann which was originally part of the medieval fortifications. However it is only a few kilometres from **Thann** itself with its ancient and magnificent Collegiate Église de St-Thiébault and a popular legend to match.

It appears that the saintly Bishop Thiébaut, having given away his entire fortune, promised his episcopal ring to his servant before he died in Italy in 1160. In trying to claim his inheritance the servant pulled off the entire thumb which he promptly regarded as a relic, hiding it in the knob of his pilgrim's staff for the long journey back home to the Netherlands. One night in Alsace he stopped to rest in a forest of fir trees, leaning his staff against one of them. When the time came to move on it seemed to have taken root just as three bright lights appeared in the upper branches of the tree. Either the Comte de Ferrette or his wife saw them from a window in the Château d'Engelbourg and, having heard the whole story, decided to build a chapel on the site. Within a remarkably short time it became a place of pilgrimage, a small village grew up round the church to cater for the needs of travellers and took the name of Thann after the fir tree. Nowadays the ceremonial Cremation des Trois Sapins takes place on 30 June each year when three fir trees are burned outside the church and the ashes collected by pilgrims and sightseers to keep as relics or souvenirs.

The present Église de St-Thiébault, sometimes described as a cathedral, started life at the end of the thirteenth century and took more than 200 years to complete. It is a most imposing structure, lavishly carved and decorated with pinnacles and statues and roofed with glazed, multi-coloured tiles. The interior is every bit as impressive. There is a rather melancholy statue of the bishop in elaborate gold-painted robes on the altar of his chapel in the oldest part of the building and another, less-imposing likeness, in the nave, designed to be carried in procession. Opposite the Lady Chapel, which has its own statue, there is a beautifully carved and painted Virgin of the Winegrowers, carrying a mischievous-looking Child hiding a bunch of grapes behind his back. The carved oak choir stalls are well worth inspecting carefully for their imaginative range of subjects, from birds and animals to finely executed little figures such as a pensive scholar, a medieval musician, a bald man in spectacles and a wide-mouthed gossip. The stained glass windows all originated in the fifteenth century but about half of them had to be restored or replaced quite recently because of damage caused by time and two World Wars.

A block or so to the north of the church, overlooking the River Thur, the Musée des Amis de Thann in the old corn market has something of interest for everyone. The ground floor is given over largely to religious artifacts while the upper galleries concentrate on such things as the history of the town, wine making, mineralogy, folklore, handicrafts, printed fabrics and recollections of two World Wars. Slightly down river, but still in the old quarter, the Tour des Sorcières is a survivor from the original fortifications and stands guard over a bridge which offers a picturesque view of the town.

On a hilltop above Thann is the ruined **Château d'Engelbourg** which changed hands several times before it was abandoned towards the end of the seventeenth century. Its more recent owners included the Habsburgs and Louis XIV of France who gave it to Cardinal Mazarin in 1648. Eventually the title passed to the Grimaldi family with the result that each ruling Prince of Monaco is also the

Seigneur de Thann. Despite its regal connections the château continued to crumble until, today, it consists of little more than a few mouldering walls and an enormous cylindrical construction, rather like a gigantic nut designed for an even more gigantic bolt. Because it looked vaguely like an eye staring out over the Thur Valley the ruins were soon nicknamed L'Œil de la Sorcière. On the opposite side of the valley there is a monument to members of the Resistance who died in World War II.

Rouffach is a prosperous village full of flowers and elderly houses

Thann has surprisingly little to offer in the way of hotels and tends to rely on its neighbours, especially Mulhouse, to provide upmarket accommodation whenever necessary. On the other hand it can suggest a wide variety of mountain inns, farms and rural hotels for cyclists and hikers on their way through the forests or up onto the high moors. A good many different sports are available in the area, ranging from tennis, riding and swimming to hang-gliding, wind-surfing, rock climbing, fishing and even skin-diving in the Kruth-Wildenstein dam. Once the winter sets in the accent is on skiing. Le

Markstein, on the Route des Crêtes, was host to the downhill skiing world cup in 1983 but is also very popular with cross-country enthusiasts.

St-Amarin, on the N66, about half way between Thann and Kruth, was known to the Romans as *Doroangus*. However, in the early seventh century a monk called Amerinus made his home in a local convent, more than 100 years before Charlemagne handed over the whole valley to the famous Benedictine abbey at Murbach, on the opposite side of Grand Ballon. The village soon began to thrive, changed its name in honour of its patron saint and set about building walls and towers. Sadly these have disappeared, having come to grief during the Thirty Years War. Nevertheless it is still an attractive little place with old houses lining the narrow lanes and fountains hidden away in secluded squares. The home of its original tribunal was used as a military hospital in 1914 but was converted later into the Musée Serret named after General Serret. The ground floor is devoted to military operations in the Vosges during World War I and the activities of the Resistance in Alsace from 1940 to 1945. Other exhibits include coins, items of sacred art, glass from the old works at Wildenstein and examples of early printed cotton manufactured in the valley. It also highlights trades like clog-making and the advantages of distilling at home. Like every other local community St-Amarin pays tribute to St John the Baptist on the Saturday nearest to 24 June when wooden towers constructed on every available hilltop are simultaneously set on fire.

The valleys of the Thur and the Doller are linked by the historic Route Maréchal Joffre, the commander whose exploits included military encounters during the Franco-Prussian War, an expedition to Timbuktu, the defence of Verdun and the Battle of the Somme. It struggles manfully for 15km (9 miles) through the mountains by way of the Col du Hundsruck before reaching Masevaux, which has nothing in particular to recommend it. From here the scenic D466 heads for the lofty Ballon d'Alsace, passing the Lac de Sewer and the Lac d'Alfred on the way. There is plenty to see for people who are prepared to explore on foot, including a waterfall called the Cascade du Rummel, statues of the Virgin and Joan of Arc and extensive views from the summit which can be reached quite easily along a well-defined path.

According to many people the most scenic road in the Haut-Rhin is the Route des Crêtes which was designed as a straight line of communication along the border between Alsace and Lorraine-Vosges during World War I. To all intents and purposes it starts from Le Bonhomme, a small skiing centre on the D415 west of Kaysersberg. Thereafter it twists and turns among the mountain peaks and valleys, pushes its way through forests between banks of ferns and past lakes and occasional winter resorts separated from each other by high passes. At the Col de la Schlucht the route is bisected by the D417, linking Munster in Alsace with Gérardmer, the main holiday playground of the Vosges. Some 2km (1 mile) further south the **Jardin d'Altitude de Haut-Chitelet** acts like a magnet on gardening enthusiasts. This large expanse of rocky outcrops is planted with some 3,000 different species of plants from mountainous regions all over the world, grouped together according to their places of origin.

This whole area has been bedevilled by wars and threats of war for centuries. Holneck, the obtrusive mountain peak on the opposite side of the road, rising to a height of 1,362m, (4,467ft) once marked the border between France and Germany. However there is nothing of military moment to be seen as the Route des Crêtes presses on through Le Markstein to pay its respects to the Grand Ballon, at 142m (466ft) the highest point in the Vosges. Anyone in need of a little exercise can leave the car at the hotel and climb up to the top where there is a monument to the Diables Bleus, the famous mountain troops, and a view which, on a clear day, is said to extend as far as the Alps.

Hereafter the road continues with enough bends to make an energetic boa constrictor envious, past the ruined Château de Freundstein and a turning off to **Vieil-Armand**, the site of a ferocious battle in World War I in which some 30,000 French and German soldiers lost their lives. There is an impressive monument to several thousand unknown combatants, tributes to both the Diables Rouges and the Chasseurs Allemands and a vestige of the German trenches. From here it is a simple matter to rejoin the Route des Crêtes or take a less demanding minor road to Wattwiller, both of which converge on Cernay for the last part of the trip to Mulhouse.

For the past 200 years or more **Mulhouse** has been a busy and prosperous industrial city with a shrewd eye for a commercial venture. It is ideally placed on the River Ill and the Canal du Rhône au Rhin with easy access to the Grand Canal d'Alsace. Switzerland is only 34km (21 miles) away while Germany is considerably closer, just across the Rhine. It has an international airport, is an important rail junction and holds a commanding position on the main highway from the Benelux countries to Switzerland, Austria and Italy. As far as tourists are concerned it has a reasonable selection of comfortable hotels, none of them very atmospheric but generally well-equipped with swimming pools, some facilities for disabled visitors and, in one case at least, a tennis court. There are plenty of restaurants, including the modest variety that are popular with university students, a sports centre, an 18-hole golf course in the vicinity and marked paths through the Tannenwald and Rheinwald forests.

The city is essentially modern with only an occasional reminder of days gone by. Most of them are within a few blocks of the Place de la Réunion although the majority of its outstanding museums are scattered around much further afield. Of these the most memorable is probably the Musée de l'Automobile on the Avenue de Colmar. It is a story that began more than half a century ago when two textile millionaires, Hans and Fritz Schlumpf, began to indulge their passion for antique cars. Their collection was such a closely guarded secret that each new acquisition was delivered by rail at night and transported to a specially selected warehouse smothered in tarpaulins. Meanwhile the textile factories the brothers had inherited continued to flourish, firstly during World War II as a result of collaboration with the Nazis and later through judicious management and government grants for new machinery. However the profits all found their way into the bottomless pit created by the brothers' obsession with motor vehicles and in 1976 they went bankrupt and fled to Basel to escape the wrath of their creditors.

The factories were seized by the government and sold off to cover some of the debts but it was several hundred employees who broke into the secret warehouse and discovered where the millions of missing francs had gone. Eventually the collection was bought by a syndicate that included the city of Mulhouse and the French Government who promptly declared it a National Monument.

The cars, some 500 altogether and all in perfect working order, are parked on either side of walkways covering a distance of more than 2km (1 mile) and lit from above by 900 art nouveau gas lamps. Among them are 123 Bugattis, the largest collection in the world, including two Royales, a limousine and the incomparable Coupé Napoléon, custom built for Ettore Bugatti in 1932. Other showstoppers are an 1878 Jacquot station wagon, more than a dozen Rolls-Royces, among them Charlie Chaplin's 1937 Phantom III, and the so-called Big Mercedes of 1939 with a top speed of 125 miles (201km) an hour. Also on view are Fangio's Maserati and the Porsche 917 that won the Le Mans 24-hour race in 1971. On the more modest side are the two-seater 'Baby' Peugeots built before 1914. The slightly earlier Panhard-Levassor limousine has a front seat that is open to the weather and an enclosed one behind whose doors and windows look as though they were inspired by an ancient stage coach. Some of the upholstery in the more luxurious cars would not look out of place in an opulent mansion while a whole variety of radiator mascots are museum pieces in their own right.

For railway enthusiasts and anyone whose interest in cars is strictly minimal, the Musée Français du Chemin de Fer, Rue Alfred de Glehn, on the far side of the Rue du Thann, is a viable alternative. Like the Musée de l'Automobile it claims to be unique and houses a collection of engines, carriages and wagons spanning more than 150 years. In the entrance hall the first to be seen is Stephenson's 1846 engine, the *Aigle*, beautifully restored to mint condition.

In the sheds behind, rolling stock of every description are lined up for inspection including a massive, steam-driven monster that can be activated with a coin in the appropriate slot. The wheels, mercifully clear of the rails, begin to turn, all the sounds associated with a typical French railway station can be heard, a whistle blows, there is a rush of steam, the train gathers speed — and then the money runs out. Among the most ornate carriages is one used by Napoléon III's aides-de-camp, one of whom appears to have been a doctor. At all events they took with them the emperor's travelling medicine chest that is so crammed with pills and potions that it is doubtful if any germ would have stood a chance. There is a carriage used by the Grand Duchess of Luxembourg until 1930, the first electric engine, dating from the turn of the century, and the famous BB 9 004 which held the world speed record for many years. In addition there are enough other items associated with railways, from original signals to a model train, to keep the average enthusiast happy for hours.

Next door to the railway museum is the Musée du Sapeur-Pompier, full of antiquated fire engines, uniforms and so on. Elsewhere a considerable amount of attention has also been given to the art of colour printing on various types of material as well as paper. The Musée de l'Impression sur Étoffes, on the Rue des Bonnes-Gens, is concerned exclusively with the history of printed fabrics since the eighteenth century. There are some magnificent examples from foreign parts, such as India and Persia, scarves and handkerchiefs that were all the rage in Europe 100 years ago and a section devoted to France in general and Alsace in particular. Also on view are various types of machines and equipment used at different times in the textile industry.

The Musée du Papier Peint, rather out on a limb near the Rue Wilson, contains well over 100,000 different documents tracing the history of paper and the developments which have taken place. There are rare colour prints from Paris that escaped the attention of the Revolutionaries in 1789 and massive vistas dating from the first part of the nineteenth century. Much of the credit is given to Jean Züber whose artistic ability was obviously matched by his patience in producing so many shades and colours.

The Place de la Réunion, at the heart of what could roughly be described as the old town, is overlooked by the sixteenth-century

Hôtel de Ville. In the course of its long life it has acquired some unexpected coats-of-arms, ranging from those of the Habsburgs to the emblems of various Swiss cantons. It has also set aside a considerable part of the building for the Musée Historique, which is certainly worth visiting. It has an archaeological section containing among its exhibits some pieces of late Stone Age jewellery. There are also collections of interesting costumes, weapons, furniture and artifacts that were once commonplace in the region, augmented by items of popular art. Children who might well get bored looking at cases of medals and coins brighten up considerably when they see the display of toys, such as dolls' houses, on the second floor.

The Temple of St-Étienne, also on the Place de la Réunion, has some fourteenth-century stained glass windows that were incorporated into the present church when its predecessor was demolished in the nineteenth century, but nothing else of any abiding interest. The Musée des Beaux-Arts in the nearby Place Guillaume-Tell falls into the same general category with some moderately viewable seventeenth- and eighteenth-century paintings. On view are works by local artists such as Henner, known mainly for his portraits, and Lehmann who died in 1953. Meanwhile, a smartish walk away, facing on to the Grand Rue, is the Musée de la Chapelle St-Jean. The building once belonged to the Knights of St John of Jerusalem and is

Fangio's victorious Maserati in the Musée de l'Automobile, Mulhouse

full of sculptures and antiquated murals as well as some elderly tombstones. The only other places worth mentioning are the tower in the Place de l'Europe, offering a comprehensive view over the city, and the large botanical garden on the far side of the Canal du Rhône au Rhin which includes the local zoo.

South of Mulhouse the Sundgau is mainly farming country, dotted with small villages and ponds filled with carp. The only community of any size is **Altkirch**, 18km (12 miles) from Mulhouse on the D432, built on a hill overlooking the valley of the Ill. It has been in existence in one form or another for about 800 years without having a great deal to show for it. The local attractions include the Hôtel de ville with its Musée Sundgauvien, whose interests are confined to the immediate area, and a church containing the twelfth-century tomb of St-Morand, the patron saint of Sundgau. The town is a popular centre with people who enjoy walking, riding and swimming, has a couple of quite acceptable *auberges* in the vicinity and provides facilities for tents and caravans.

Ferrette, 19km (12 miles) to the south, is dominated by a ruined château that was once the home of the Counts of Ferrette, whereas **Oberlarg** has both the remains of Morimont castle and some quite modest prehistoric grottoes. Anyone interested in fishing is advised to try their luck at Lucelle, just down the road.

Motorists with some time in hand to explore the surrounding area might well choose any of the minor or secondary roads that head westwards across country between the N19 and the D419 in the direction of **Belfort**. This is an historic town commanding the important passage between the Vosges and the Jura known as the Gap of Belfort. As a strategic road and rail centre on the River Savoureuse the town has attracted a great deal of unwelcome attention, particularly during the Franco-Prussian War and again in the closing stages of World War II. As a result, very few of its architectural landmarks are more than about 250 years old, the only relic from its early days being the corn exchange, now converted into the Jules Heidet school.

Towards the end of the seventeenth century Maréchal Vauban took Belfort in hand, redesigning it with wider roads and rather stereotyped houses surrounded by high defensive walls. At this time there were only two entrances, the Porte de France that was demolished in 1892 and the Porte de Brisach, reached these days across a narrow causeway over a grass-filled moat. The focal point is the citadelle, guarded by Bartholdi's magnificent stone lion commemorating the siege of 1870/71. The extremely businesslike fortress that looks more like a barracks than anything else is well-equipped with underground vaults and tunnels and contains a reasonably informative history museum. The Cathédrale St-Christophe, on the Place d'Armes in the shadow of the citadelle, was completed in 1750 and is understandably proud of its splendid, decorative organ, installed at the same time but enlarged and improved upon in 1848 and again in 1966. The nearby Hôtel de Ville is slightly more photogenic and older by some 26 years.

Belfort makes up for its lack of historic buildings by providing a variety of alternative attractions, most of them in the modern town on the other side of the river. There is a Baroque-style theatre overlooking the water, some most attractive gardens off the Avenue Jean-Jaurés, the Fontaine de Guy de Rougemont with its nine lofty multi-coloured pillars and shopping precincts like the Faubourg de France. When it comes to sport the facilities are many and varied, including a skating rink, several tennis courts, swimming pools, footpaths and cycle tracks. Rock climbers can be seen practising on the rocky cliffs below the fortress while sailing and windsurfing enthusiasts make for the Etang des Forges on the north-eastern outskirts.

Belfort is particularly well supplied with hotels and restaurants, both in and outside the town. Among them are the Grand Hotel du Lion on the Rue Clemenceau, ☎ 84 21 17 00, the Château Servin in the Rue du Général Négrier which is an excellent restaurant with a few rooms for guests, and the Mercure Belfort-Danjoutin, ☎ 84 21 55 01 some 3km (2 miles) to the south on the N19. From Belfort there are three main roads linking its rather limited territory with Alsace — the D419 runs due east to Altkirch, the N83 heads north-east past Cernay to Colmar, a distance of 74km (46 miles) while the A36 *autoroute* is the most direct link with Mulhouse 42km (26 miles) away.

Additional Information

Places to Visit

BAS-RHIN

Fleckenstein
Château
Near Lembach
Open: all day from March to November.

Haguenau
Musée Alsacien
Rue de la Moder
Open: mornings and afternoons but afternoons only on Sundays and holidays. Closed Tuesdays.

Musée Historique
Rue Maréchal Foch
Open: mornings and afternoons but afternoons only on Saturdays and Sundays. Closed Tuesdays and holidays.

Le Haut Barr
Musée du Télégraphe Claude-Chappe
Near the château
Open: mornings and afternoons mid-June to mid-September.

Kintzheim
Montagne des Singes
Open: mornings and afternoons
April to mid-September. Wednesdays, Saturdays, Sundays and
holidays only mid-September to
mid-November.

Volerie des Aigles
At the castle
Open: each afternoon April to mid-
September. Wednesdays, Satur-
days, Sundays and holidays only
mid-September to mid-November.

Lembach
Ouvrage du Four à Chaux
1km (½ mile) away
Open: for guided tours 9am,
10.30am, 2pm, 4pm and 5pm July
and August. Additional tours if
required on Saturdays, Sundays
and holidays.

Neuwiller-lès-Saverne
Chapels in the Church
In order to view contact the curate
at 5 Cour du Chapitre.

La Petite-Pierre
Château
Open: mornings and afternoons
June to September but closed on
Saturday mornings. Sunday and
holiday afternoons only April,
May, October and to 11 November.

Magazin
In the ramparts
Open: mornings and afternoons
July and August. Closed Tuesdays.

Musée du Sceau Alsacien
In the Chapelle St-Louis
Open: mornings and afternoons
July and August. Otherwise
Saturday and Sunday mornings
and afternoons and during school
holidays.

Rosheim
Église St-Pierre-et-St-Paul
If it is closed enquire at the
pâtisserie opposite.

St-Jean-Saverne
Chapelle St-Michel
2km (1 mile) from the town
Open: Sunday afternoons only.

Saverne
Jardin Botanique
About 3km (2 miles) from the town
Open: afternoons June to August
but Sundays and holidays only in
June.

Museum
In the château
Open: mornings and afternoons,
except on Tuesdays, July and
August. Mornings and afternoons
Sundays and holidays only May,
June and September.

Roseraie
Open: mornings and afternoons
mid-June to end of September.

Sélestat
Bibliothèque Humaniste
Place Gambetta
Open: mornings and afternoons.
Closed Saturday afternoons,
Sundays and holidays.

Strasbourg
Barrage Vauban
Orientation table open all day. Free
access from November to February.

Cathédrale Notre-Dame
Horloge Astronomique
Conducted tours at 12.30pm.

Cathedral Spire
Open: all day. Enquire at the
bottom of the tower in the Place du
Château. Cathedral *son et lumière*
each evening at 9pm mid-April to
the end of September.

Église St-Guillaume
Over the river beyond the Pont Ste-
  Madeleine
If closed enquire at 2 Rue St-
Guillaume or ☎ 35 16 79

Église St-Pierre-le-Jeune
Open: mornings and afternoons
from Easter to All Saints' Day, but
closed on Sunday mornings.

Museums
All museums, except the one listed
below, are open mornings and
afternoons April to September.
Weekday afternoons and Sunday
mornings and afternoons October
to March. Closed Tuesdays, Good
Friday, 1 May, 1 November, 25
December and New Years Day.

Musée Zoologique de l'Université
Open: mornings and afternoons on
Wednesdays and Sundays.
Otherwise mornings only. Closed
Tuesdays except April to Septem-
ber and all holidays.

Palais de l'Europe
Open: mornings and afternoons for
pre-arranged tours: ☎ 61 49 61.
Closed Saturdays and Sundays
November to March, on holidays
and when the European Parliament
is in session.

River Trips
From the pier near the Château des
  Rohan
Regular services all day from mid-
March to end of October. Evening
trips to see the illuminations June
to September.
☎ 32 75 25 for reservations.

Strasbourg From The Air
From Aérodrome du Polygone
Reached along the Route du
Polygone in the south-east of the
city.

Le Struthof
Nazi Concentration Camp
Guided tours each morning and
afternoon. Closed 24 December and
1 January.

Wissembourg
Musée Westercamp
Near the Promenade des Remparts
Open: mornings and afternoons.
Closed Sunday mornings, Wednes-
days and throughout January.

Woerth
Musée du 6 Août 1870
Open: mornings and afternoons for
guided tours April to October. Oth-
erwise mornings and afternoons on
Saturdays and Sundays only.

HAUT-RHIN
Altkirch
Musée Sundgauvien
In the Hôtel de Ville
Open: afternoons only July to
September. Closed Mondays and
holidays. Open Sunday afternoons
only October to June.

Cernay
Museum
In the Porte de Thann
Open: Wednesday and Friday
afternoons July and August.

Steam Train
From Cernay to Sentheim
Operates on Sundays and holidays.
☎ 82 31 01

Colmar
Musée Bartholdi
Rue des Marchands
Open: mornings and afternoons
April to October. Mornings and af-
ternoons Wednesdays and Saturdays
only November to March.

Église des Dominicians
Rue des Serruriers
Open: all day April to mid-
November.

Église St-Matthieu
In the Grand Rue
Open: at Easter as well as mornings
and afternoons from mid-June to
mid-September. Closed Sundays.

Musée d'Unterlinden
Place Unterlinden
Open: mornings and afternoons.
Closed Tuesdays, November to
March, 1 January, 1 November and
25 December.

Ensisheim
Musée Historique
In the Hôtel de Ville
Open: mornings and afternoons.
Closed Saturdays and Sundays.

Gunsbach
Musée Albert Schweitzer
Open: for guided tours mornings
and afternoons.

Haut-Koenigsbourg
Château
North-west of St-Hippolyte
Open: mornings and afternoons.
Closed on holidays and during
January.

Jardin d'Altitude de Haut-Chitelet
Near the Col de la Schlucht
Open: all day from June to mid-
October.

Kaysersberg
Musée Albert Schweitzer
Rue Genéral de Gaulle
Open: at Easter as well as mornings
and afternoons May to October.

Chapelle St-Michel
Adjacent to the church
If closed enquire at the tourist
office in the Hôtel de Ville.

Musée Communal
Rue Général de Gaulle
Open: at Easter and Whitsun,
mornings and afternoons July and
August, mornings and afternoons
on Sundays and holidays only
during June, September and
October.

Kientzheim
Musée du Vin Alsace
Open: mornings and afternoons
July to September.

Mulhouse
Musée de l'Automobile
Avenue de Colmar
Open: all day. Closed Tuesdays, 25
December and 1 January.

Parc Zoologique et Botanique
Open: all day.

Musée de la Chapelle St-Jean
Grand Rue
Open: mornings and afternoons
May to September. Closed
Tuesdays, 1 May, Whit Monday, 14
July.

Musée des Beaux-Arts
Place Guillaume-Tell
Open: mornings and afternoons.
Closed Tuesdays, Whit Monday, 14
July, 1 and 11 November, 25 and 26
December.

Musée du Sapeur-Pompier
Rue Jose Hofer
Open: all day. Closed 1 January
and 25 and 26 December.

Musée Historique
Attached to the Hôtel de Ville
Open: mornings and afternoons as
well as Thursday evenings mid-
June to September. Closed
Tuesdays and holidays.

Musée de l'Impression sur Étoffes
Rue des Bonnes-Gens
Open: mornings and afternoons.
Closed Tuesdays and holidays.

Musée du Papier Peint
Off Rue Wilson
Open: mornings and afternoons.
Closed Tuesdays and holidays.

Musée Français du Chemin de Fer
Rue Alfred de Glehn
Open: 9am-6pm April to September. 9am-5pm October to March.
Closed 1 January and 25 and 26 December.

Neuf-Brisach
Steam Train
From Neuf-Brisach to
    Marckolsheim
Operates Saturdays, Sundays and holidays only during May, June and September.
☎ 82 31 01

Musée Vauban
Porte de Belfort
Open: for guided tours mornings and afternoons. Closed Tuesdays.

Riquewihr
Musée de la Société d'Archéologie
In the Dolder
Open: during the Easter holidays and mornings and afternoons during July and August. From after Easter until the end of June and during September and October only open on Saturday afternoons and Sundays.

Musée d'Histoire des P.T.T. d'Alsace
In the château
Open: mornings and afternoons April to mid-November. Closed Tuesdays except during July and August.

Tour des Voleurs
Rue et Cout des Juifs
Keeps the same hours as the Musée de la Société d'Archéologie.

Ste-Marie-aux-Mines
Musée Minéralogique
Open: mornings and afternoons during July and August.

Schoppenwihr Parc Naturel
Open: mornings and afternoons July to mid-September but afternoons only from Easter to the end of June and mid-September until All Saints Day.

Thann
Musée des Amis de Thann
Overlooking the river
Open: mornings and afternoons mid-May to September.

Église de St-Thiébaut
In order to see the stalls enquire at the presbytery or the Tourist Office.

Ungersheim
Écomusée de Haut-Alsace
Open: daily throughout the year.

Vieil-Armand
The National Monument
Open: mornings and afternoons April to October. There is no entrance fee on 14 July or 11 November.

Tourist Information Offices

BAS-RHIN

Barr
Hôtel de Ville
Syndicat d'Initiative
☎ 88 08 94 24

Dambach-la-Ville
Syndicat d'Initiative
Place Marché and the Hôtel de Ville
Open: July and August
☎ 88 92 41 05

Haguenau
Office de Tourisme
Place J-Thierry
☎ 88 73 30 41

Lembach
Syndicat d'Initiative
Route Bitche
☎ 88 94 43 16

Molsheim
Office de Tourisme
Place Hôtel de Ville
☎ 88 38 11 61

Niederbronn-les-Bains
Office de Tourisme
Place Hôtel de Ville
☎ 88 09 17 00

Obernai
Office de Tourisme
Chapelle du Beffroi
☎ 88 95 64 13

Rosheim
Office de Tourisme
In the Mairie
Open: mid-June to mid-September.
☎ 88 50 40 10

Saverne
Office de Tourisme
Château des Rohan
☎ 88 91 80 47

Sélestat
Office de Tourisme
Boulevard Général Leclerc
☎ 88 92 02 66

Villé
Office de Tourisme
Hôtel de Ville
☎ 88 57 11 57

Wissembourg
Office de Tourisme
Hôtel de Ville
☎ 88 94 10 11

HAUT-RHIN

Cernay
Office de Tourisme
Rue Latouche
Open: June to September.
☎ 89 75 50 35

Colmar
Office de Tourisme
Rue Unterlinden
☎ 89 41 02 29

Kaysersberg
Office de Tourisme
In the Hôtel de Ville
☎ 89 78 22 78

Mulhouse
Office de Tourisme
Avenue Maréchal Foch
☎ 89 45 68 31
and Avenue Colmar from June to
October.

Neuf-Brisach
Office de Tourisme
Place d'Armes
Open: mid-June to mid-September.
☎ 89 72 56 66
Out of season enquire at the
Mairie.
☎ 89 72 51 68

Ribeauvillé
Office de Tourisme
Grand Rue
☎ 89 73 62 22

Riquewihr
Office de Tourisme
Rue Genéral de Gaulle
Open: April to November.
☎ 89 47 80 80

Thann
Office de Tourisme
Place Joffre
Open: June to September.
☎ 89 37 96 20

Champagne & Alsace-Lorraine Fact File

Accommodation

There is no shortage of accommodation in France except in popular holiday resorts at the height of the season when it may be essential to book in advance. However, this is when the major cities are less busy than usual and therefore the problem is not so apparent. Once across the Channel tourist offices can usually supply some local addresses, but only the ones also known as 'Accueil de France' will actually make bookings, although not for more than 8 days ahead and then only for visitors who call in personally.

There are many different types of accommodation from expensive and luxurious to cheap and rather basic, with several different categories in between; a fact which applies as much to hotels as it does to private houses and campsites.

Hotels

Hotels are nationally inspected and supervised. They are graded with stars into five categories: one star is simple but comfortable, four stars (L) is luxury. Prices rise according to category. Rates are usually given for two, and single rooms, if you can find them, may not be much cheaper than double. A third bed will normally cost about 30 per cent extra, though many hotel chains now offer a free bed for a child under 12 in the same room as the parents.

Breakfast is not usually included in the price of the room. Most hotels offer special rates for *pension complète* (room with full meals) or *demi-pension* (room, breakfast and one other meal). You cannot by law be refused a room if you do not want *pension* arrangements, though some hoteliers may expect you to take them. If you do, check that the *pension* menu offers you the same choice as other restaurant menus. You can eat in hotel restaurants without staying there. The good average hotels are usually perfectly acceptable but those that are rated as 'quite comfortable' may or may not live up to this description. On the other hand, the ones in the 'modest comfort' bracket can sometimes be delightful. Hotels belonging to several well-known international chains can be found in most major cities, whereas the 'Relais & Chateau' group members are more likely to be mansions in the country or attached to small villages.

A good many privately-owned hotels throughout France have banded together, with official blessing, to form associations like the Hôtellerie Familiale, whose sign is a blue road with yellow markings extended to form the letters HF. However the best known examples are the Logis de France and the Auberges de France which are identified by a yellow stone fireplace against a green shield. The former are mainly classified as one or two-star hotels, whereas the latter have too few rooms to qualify for the official star ratings.

Lists of approved hotels are produced by the French Government Tourist Office, and by local Syndicats d'Initiative. Bookings can be made direct to the hotel by phone (though you may have to send a deposit, or *acompte*, which you may lose if you cancel), or through a group central booking service for hotels in a chain. Book well ahead and remember to confirm your booking on your day of arrival if you are likely to arrive late (after 7pm).

Other Types Of Accommodation

The most popular type of non-hotel accommodation in France is the *gîte*. This is a self-catering holiday home in or near an inland country village. It may be a small cottage, village house, flat in the owner's house or part of a farm; the owner will not be living in it at the time, but may be on hand nearby. *Gîtes* are rented for a week or longer (two weeks in peak season) and are reasonably priced. This is one reason for their popularity, and why you should book early. They are all inspected and graded, and are usually in good condition. They are often in beautiful countryside, but sometimes remote from civilisation.

Not to be confused with *gîtes* are *gîtes d'etape* (short-stay centres for those on a walking or horseback tour) and *gîtes d'enfants* (centres for groups of children on an outdoor activities holiday). These are really types of hostel, like the *auberges de jeunesse*, or youth hostels. These are worth considering for a short stay: they normally take younger adults as well as children, and they often provide meals and beds, usually in bunkhouses. Another possibility for budget accommodation is the *chambre d'hôte*. This is a room with bed and breakfast in the house of a family in residence, usually in the country and often on a farm. It is a good way of meeting the local people and sampling their produce.

Tourist information centres produce the pamphlet *Youth Welcome* listing youth hostels (*auberge de jeunesse*). Other useful addresses are:

Fédération Unie des Auberges de Jeunesse
27 Rue Pajol
75118 Paris
☎ 42 41 59 00

UCRIF (Union des Centres de Recontres
   Internationales de France)
21 Rue Béranger
75003 Paris
☎ 42 77 08 65

Camping and Caravanning
If you take your own accommodation with you, in the form of a tent, trailer-tent, caravan or camping-car, you have the choice of camping *au sauvage* (in the wild) or on a camp site. Many French people do the former, but make sure the *camping sauvage* is not *interdit* (prohibited), and get permisson from the local farmer or landowner. He may make a small charge for this, but should provide in return access to some basic facilities like running water. He may indeed make regular provision for *camping à la ferme* (camping on small farm sites) in which case he should provide toilets and washing facilities and may have farm produce for sale.

French camp-sites are well organised, regularly inspected and classified with stars into five categories (including ungraded). Stars are nearly always displayed at the site entrance, and are a good guide to the amenities offered, though this does not necessarily mean that the site will be to your taste. At the top of the range, four-star *grand confort* sites should be spacious and attractively landscaped, with your own clearly-marked pitch, an electrical hook-up, and comprehensive amenities, including a restaurant and hot food takeaway, bar, supermarket, laundry, full washing facilities with free hot water, and sports facilities. Some of these are in the Castels et Camping Caravaning chain, whose sites are attractively located in the grounds of châteaux or other historic buildings. Further down the range, a two-star site will still offer basic amenities, which should include hot water and a shop or *buvette* with basic food requirements.

Maximum and minimum daily temperatures

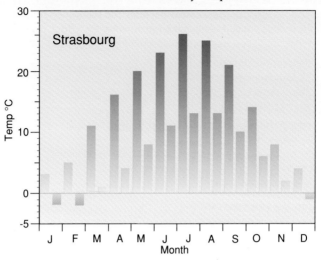

Strasbourg

Average monthly rainfall

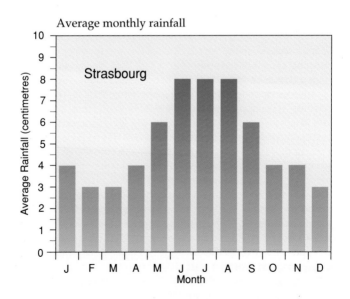

Strasbourg

The star grading is not always a reliable guide to the quality of a site. It refers to the amenities the site offers, not to the way it is run. If a site is badly managed (too lax in enforcing the rules, unhelpful and impersonal service) it can still have a high grading, though it may lose this eventually.

Climate

The climate in north-eastern France varies quite considerably, depending on the area and the time of year. It can be hot in mid-summer, although seldom unbearably so, and cold enough for snow up in the mountains during the winter when ski lifts are in operation. The best times for touring are in the spring while all the flowers are out and in autumn when the trees and vineyards are starting to change colour.

Currency and Credit Cards

Visitors may take unlimited currency into France and only bank notes to the value of 50,000FF or more need be declared if they are likely to be re-exported. When shopping around for favourable exchange rates, take into account any commission charges that may be added. The French *franc* (abbreviated F or FF) is divided into 100 *centimes*. Current coins include 5, 10, 20 and 50 *centime* pieces as well as 1, 2, 5 and 10 *franc* pieces. Bank notes come in denominations of 20, 50, 100, 200 and 500 francs.

When changing things like travellers' cheques it is as well to remember that banks give the best rate of exchange. Travellers' cheques in French francs cost more than Sterling ones initially, but may offset a poor rate of exchange and high commission charges for changing your cheques in France. Do not let anyone charge you for changing franc travellers' cheques — ask in advance, and try another bank if they do.

Most major credit cards, such as Access, American Express and Visa, also known as Carte Bleue, are accepted by the majority of large hotels, restaurants, and some shops and garages. However there are exceptions, so if there is no logo on display it is as well to enquire in advance. Eurocheques and travellers' cheques may also be accepted but in out-of-the-way places it would be wise to have adequate French *francs* as well.

Customs Regulations

Customs regulations no longer apply between EC countries in the normal course of events. However this facility does not apply to visitors from other countries, who should enquire about the prevailing rules and regulations before leaving home.

Disabled Facilities

France is becoming increasingly aware of the needs of disabled visitors. Several towns set aside parking bays for drivers who display disabled discs and some hotels have rooms on the ground floor, but contrary to expectations, not all motels provide easy access for people in wheelchairs. The French Government Tourist Office issue a special information sheet for disabled visitors to France. This is available on application with a stamped addressed envelope.

The Liaison Committee for the Transport of Disabled Persons (Comité de Liaison pour le Transport des Personnes Handicapées) 34 Avenue Marceau Paris 8e and the Ministry of Equipment, Housing, Transport and the Sea (Ministère de l'Equipment, du Logement, des Transports et de la Mer) 92055 Paris La Defense Cédex 04 publish a transport guide for the disabled.

The French National Committee of Liaison for the Re-Education of the Disabled (Comité National Français de Liaison pour la Réadaptation des Handicapées) 38 Bld Raspail, Paris 7e sells two guides for the use of people with a handicap: *Paris-Guide to Cinemas, Theatres, Concerts* and *Paris-Museums, Libraries, Cultural Centres and Workshops*.

A list of *gîtes* with accommodation for disabled travellers and regional numbers of the APF (Association des Paralyses de France) can be obtained from the central office at:

17 Boulevard Auguste-Blanqui
75013 Paris
☎ 140 78 69 00

Other useful addresses to contact for information are:

Red Cross	Royal Association for
Croix Rouge Paris	Disability and Rehabilitation
1 Place Henri Dunant	25 Mortimer Street
75384 Paris	London W1N 8AB
☎ 1 44 43 11 00	☎ 071 637 5400

Electricity

France operates on 220 volts but adaptors will be needed by anyone who uses anything other than continental two-pin plugs at home.

Embassies and Consulates

Foreign Embassies and Consulates in France are:

UK
Embassy
35 Rue du Faubourg
   Saint-Honoré
75008 Paris
☎ 42 66 91 42

Consulate
16 Rue d'Anjou
75008 Paris
(same telephone number)

USA
Embassy-Chancellery
2 Avenue Gabriel
75008 Paris
☎ 42 96 12 02

Australia
Embassy and Consulate
4 Rue Jean-Rey
75015 Paris
☎ 40 59 33 00

Canada
Embassy-Chancellery
35 av Montaigne
75008 Paris
☎ 47 23 01 01

The Foreign Office leaflet *Get it Right Before you Go* gives advice on how to behave in France, and provides information about the services offered by the Consulate. This is obtainable from the French Government Tourist Office (see page 177-178).

Festivals

North-eastern France has its full quota of fairs, fêtes and festivals, some of them religious or traditional while others are simply designed as entertainments or are in connection with a particular activity, trade or industry. There are too many minor events to mention but a few of the most important ones are worth remembering:

January — Feast of St-Vincent at different places in Champagne-Ardenne.

March — Carnival in Châlons-sur-Marne.

Easter — Fête des Champs Golots at Épinal.

May — Lily of the Valley festivals in Chaource and Neuf-Brisach. Festival de Théâtre in Nancy.

June — Music Festival in Strasbourg. Fête de Jeanne d'Arc in Reims. Festival de la Rose in Saverne.

August — Performances at the Théâtre du Peuple (the oldest people's theatre in France) in Bussang. Foire aux Vins in Colmar. Procession of Flowers in Sélestat. Fête de la Mirabelle in Metz.

September — Festival of Strolling Players in Ribeauvillé. European Festival in Strasbourg.

October — World Marionette Festival at Charleville-Mézières. Fête des Vendanges at Barr.

December — The Fête de Ste-Odile. Celebrations and pilgrimages in honour of the patron saint of Alsace. Christmas celebrations in many places including Strasbourg, Metz, Nancy and Thionville.

Health Care

British visitors in possession of an E111 form, obtained from the post office before leaving, are entitled to medical care in France. Travellers from other countries outside the EC should make sure that they have adequate cover for the duration of their visits. Some hotels with telephones in the bedrooms provide emergency numbers for use at night but, failing this, anyone in need of assistance should dial 19. In out-of-the-way places it may be necessary to contact the local police. In the case of minor ailments a qualified chemist in the local pharmacy, which is easy to identify by its green cross, can often deal with the problem on the spot or, if a doctor is needed, will know how to find one. Many familiar medicines can be bought at the pharmacy but, if not, the local equivalent is frequently just as good, and sometimes even better.

Insurance

Basic car insurance is obligatory throughout the EC countries but it is as well to discuss possible extra cover with your insurance company. If necessary make sure that the policies related to such things and jewellery and expensive cameras are valid for the trip, in addition to which it is possible to take out short-term policies, including extra health cover, for the duration of a holiday.

Language

Although a good many French people speak a certain amount of English, some of them extremely fluently, any attempt to return the compliment is much appreciated. *Bonjour Madame* or *Monsieur* in the morning accompanied by a smile, *au revoir* when leaving and *merci* instead of 'thank you' make a good start. Thereafter a small dictionary comes in useful and so do some local children who most probably learn English at school. Motorists in out-of-the-way places in need of fuel can use sign language or say *le plein s'il vous plait*, in other words, 'please fill it up'. In a restaurant *table d'hôte* or 'menu' is a set meal whereas *à la carte* refers to items ordered separately; *plat du jour* is the main dish of the day while *plat du terroir* indicates a local speciality. It is also as well to know that *interdit* means prohibited and no smoking is *défense de fumer*.

Maps

The *Michelin Motoring Atlas of France* is recommended for its detail (1:200,000). If you do buy the Michelin atlas, make sure you get the spiral-bound version, as it is more durable. It contains a planning map, a map of French departments, plans of major towns and cities and a gazetteer.

For route planning, the *Michelin Map 911* is invaluable. It contains information on motorways and alternative routes, distances and journey times, 24-hour service stations, and peak travel periods to avoid. This can be supplemented by the red *Michelin Map 989*, an excellent road map for getting from A to B. Its scale is l:1,000,000, and it lists all the N (National) and many D (Departmental) roads. It also marks the French *Départements* in black and the detailed Michelin map numbers in blue. The AA also produces a clear and uncluttered road map of France (1:1,000,000), with a folding/colour coding system and showing toll and toll-free motorways. This is also available in 'Glovebox Atlas' form. The AA/Baedeker map is slightly more detailed (1:750,000) and has city-centre plans of main towns. The French equivalent of the British Ordnance Survey map is the IGN, or *Institut Géographique National*, with a scale of 1:100,000. Even larger-scale maps are the IGN Blue (1:25,000). These are useful for walkers and climbers, showing contours, footpaths and many other details. The IGN also has a range of planning maps.

Measurements

The metric system is used in France. Conversions are:

1kilo (1,000 grams) = 2.2lb
1 litre = 1¾ pints
4.5 litres = 1 gallon
8km = 5 miles

Opening Hours

Opening and closing hours in France are fairly uniform but those in country areas may vary slightly from their counterparts in the larger towns and cities.

Banks (*banque*) are open on weekdays from 9am to 12noon and again from 2-4pm but they are closed for the day on either Saturday or Monday. They also close early on the day before a public holiday.

Post Offices (*Bureau de Poste*) in general are open from 8am to 7pm on weekdays but close for the weekend at 12noon on Saturday. However it is quite possible that a small country post office may also take about an hour off for lunch during the week. To avoid waiting around it is useful to know that stamps (*timbre*) can be bought from newsagents and are also available in some hotels.

Shopping hours can vary quite considerably so it is only possible to give a general guideline on what to expect. The usual practice is to open at about 9am, close for lunch at 12noon, reopen at 2pm and close for the night at any time between 6.30 and 7.30pm. Exceptions to the rule are large shops in the cities, some of which do not close for lunch, and supermarkets which tend to stay open all day and may well not close until 9pm or 10pm. A great many shops of all descriptions are closed on Mondays, either in the morning or for the whole day. Some food shops, especially bakers, open for a few hours on Sunday mornings and occasionally it is possible to find a Sunday morning market.

Museums follow a fairly uniform pattern although there can be some unexpected variations. On the whole they open in the mornings and afternoons on weekdays, part of Saturday and Sunday, close one day a week and sometimes on holidays. Quite a few small villages have their own little museums which keep almost-normal hours that can be altered without notice, depending largely on the time of year.

Churches are a law unto themselves. The large, famous ones are quite predictable but in outlying areas they may well be kept locked and so it is necessary to find someone with a key. It could be a warden, someone at the *mairie* (town hall or village hall) or the owner of the local shop.

Passports and Visas

British Nationals, and visitors from EC countries, the USA, Canada, New Zealand and a number of other countries, do not require a visa when visiting France for stays of up to 3 months. British Nationals require either a full British Passport, a Visitor's Passport (valid one year) or a British Excursion Document (valid for one month for trips of up to 60 hours at any one time — obtainable from Post Offices).

Public Holidays

There are eleven public holidays in France when all the banks, administrative offices, several museums and other places of interest are closed but an occasional shop and the majority of restaurants remain open. They are:

New Year's Day
Easter Monday
Labour Day — 1 May
Ascension Day — Six weeks after Easter
VE Day — 8 May
Whit Monday — 10 days after Ascension Day
Bastille Day — 14 July
Assumption Day — 15 August
All Saints Day — 1 November
Armistice Day — 11 November
Christmas Day — 25 December

In addition, several places observe their own individual holidays such as their Patron Saint's Day, a traditional festival, a wine fair or some other local celebration.

Sports and Pastimes

Climbing
A certain amount of climbing is possible in Alsace. The best places

to go are the Princess Emma Rocks near Champ du Feu, the Neuntelstein Rocks at La Rothlach, both in the Bas-Rhin, and two or three sites in the Hohneck Massif further south, below the Col de la Schlucht.

Cycling

Cycling is very popular throughout north-eastern France. The countryside is well-suited to both long and short trips on bicycles which can be hired at some railway stations and at centres where organised excursions are arranged for visitors. There are a variety of clearly marked cycle tracks. Information can be obtained from the local tourist offices while an all-in cycling holiday in the Bas-Rhin is available through the Association pour le Développement des Vosges du Nord, Maison du Parc, F67290 La Petite Pierre ☎ (33) 88 70 46 55.

Fishing

Licences, either one-day or seasonal, are required throughout the area where the rivers and lakes are amply supplied with trout, pike, pike-perch, perch and graylings. Apart from the various tourist offices, information is available from the Fédération Départementale des Associations Agréées de Pêche et de Pisciculture, 52 Rue d'Arches, 08000 Charleville-Mézières; 10-12 Rue François Gentil, 10000 Troyes; 32 Rue des Lombards, 51250 Sermaize-les-Bains; or 24 Rue de la Tour Mongeard, BP.61, 52002 Chaumont cedex. In Alsace the address for the same association is 2 Rue de Niederbronn, Strasbourg or 55 Rue des Vergers, Mulhouse.

Flying

In the unlikely event of a visitor planning to spend the holiday learning to fly or to glide, information on beginners' courses is available from the aero-clubs in Strasbourg, Colmar, Mulhouse, Haguenau and Sélestat.

Golf

There are rather fewer golf courses in north-eastern France than in some other parts of the country such as Aquitaine. However the game is growing in popularity all the time and new courses are being added which intend to offer temporary membership to visiting players, in some cases with the proviso that they have a handicap. In the meantime there are courses — mostly 18-hole — at Chaource, Nancy, Mulhouse, Reims, Strasbourg and Vittel. Full information can be obtained from the Fédération de Golf, 69

Avenue Victor-Hugo, 75116 Paris ☎ 45 00 43 72. Mini-golf is available in several other places throughout the area such as Charleville-Mézières, Seltz and Niederbronn-les-Bains.

Riding
Riding is an extremely popular pastime throughout the region and there are any number of equestrian centres, riding stables and pony clubs open to visitors. In addition to short trips into the surrounding countryside quite a few longer, organised excursions are available, especially in the mountains of the Vosges and the Ardennes. Full details can be obtained by writing to ANTE, 15 Rue de Bruxelles, 75009 Paris ☎ 42 81 42 82. There are special bridle paths, particularly in Alsace where some of the centres provide carriage rides for less energetic or inexperienced visitors.

Tennis
Tennis courts are available in most of the larger tourist centres and holiday resorts and are included in the various sports complexes. A number of hotels, usually those in the upper price bracket with enough space in the grounds, provide tennis for their guests but in many cases this facility is reserved for residents only.

Walking
Opportunities exist for short strolls, energetic rambles and long distance hiking throughout the region. There are literally several hundred miles of marked paths, often linking small villages, quite apart from the *Sentiers de Grande Randonnée* which enable determined walkers to set off from almost any given point and carry on well beyond the national frontiers. Detailed information about the Grandes Randonnées and the appropriate maps is obtainable from the Comité National des Sentiers de Grande Randonnée, 92 Rue de Clignancourt, 75883 Paris Cedex 18 ☎ 42 59 60 40. For less ambitious hikers who only want to explore the Vosges, small-scale maps are available from the Club Vosgien, 4 Rue de la Douane, Strasbourg.

Water Sports
There are very few water sports which cannot be enjoyed in north-eastern France due to all the lakes, rivers and canals as well as the resorts that have grown up to take advantage of them. Opportunities abound for trying out a canoe or a rowing boat, sailing, hiring a pedalo or getting the necessary permit to drive a motor boat. Windsurfing and waterskiing are equally popular and so is

swimming in the lakes and rivers as well as in the numerous swimming pools, some of which are heated.

Winter Sports

Winter sports in north-eastern France are necessarily confined to the Vosges where the main centres are La Bresse, Gérardmer and St-Maurice-sur-Moselle. The resorts are not in the same league as those in the Alps, but there are opportunities for both downhill and cross-country skiing, custom-built hotels, ski lifts and ski runs but no cable cars so far. There is also comparable skiing in the Jura mountains and details can be obtained from the tourist offices or from the Office de Tourisme Régional, Place de la Première Armée Française, 25000, Besançon.

Telephones

Telephoning France from the UK, you start with the international access code (010 33). There are no French area codes. For Paris city and Greater Paris dial 010 331 plus 8 digits. For rest of country dial 010 33 plus 8 digits.

Telephoning the UK from France, you dial 19, wait until the continuous tone recurs, then dial 44 followed by your STD code minus the first 0, and then your number, eg 19-44-21-345-2850. To phone the USA from France 19-1, Canada 19-1, Australia 19-61 followed by the telephone number.

Cheap rates give you 50 per cent extra time: on weekdays between 10.30pm and 8am, and at weekends starting 2pm on Saturdays.

Phonecards, called *télécarte*, operate in most booths. You can buy them from post offices, tobacconists, newsagents, and where advertised on telephone booths. Buy them in the UK from Voyages Vacances Int, 34 Savile Row, London W1X 1AG ☎ 071 287 3171.

Incoming calls can be received at phone boxes with a blue bell sign shown.

Emergency Numbers

Fire 18; Police 17; Operator 13; Directory Enquiries 12.

Theme Holidays

Theme holidays are becoming increasingly popular with more and more varieties being added to the list. At the moment they include arts and traditions, regional cooking, explorations on horseback, guided rambles with the emphasis on history and wild life and even trips in a flat-bottomed boat through the meadows and marshes of the Great Ried Plain of Alsace. Further information can be obtained, and reservations made, through the Loisirs Accueil, 7 Place des Meuniers, F67000 Strasbourg ☎ (33) 88 75 56 50. For information about similar opportunities available in Champagne-Ardenne the best plan is to write to one of the main tourist boards, namely:

Comitée Départemental de
  Tourisme des Ardennes
24 Place Ducale
08000 Charleville-Mézières
☎ 24 56 06 08

Comité Départemental du
  Tourisme de La Marne
2 bis Boulevard Vaubécourt
5100 Châlons-sur-Marne
☎ 26 68 37 52

Comité Départemental du
  Tourisme de l'Aube
Hôtel du Département, B.P.394
10026 Troyes cedex
☎ 25 42 50 91

Comité Départemental du
  Tourisme et du Thermalisme
  de Haute-Marne
Centre Administratif
Départemental, B.P.509
52011 Chaumont cedex
☎ 25 32 87 70

Tipping

The equivalent of VAT and, usually, service charges are added automatically to the bill so it is cheaper to pay for extras like tea or drinks than charge them to the number of your room. However, anyone giving a personal service, like guides, church caretakers, cloakroom attendants, theatre and cinema usherettes, taxi drivers and people doing similar jobs will certainly expect a tip. In other cases, such as hotel and restaurant staff, a small *pourboire* in recognition of particularly good service, or for any other reason, will always be appreciated.

Tourist Information Centres

There are tourist information centres in all the big towns and cities as well as in several of the smaller places. They may be called Office de Tourisme or Syndicat d'Initiative, have their own offices or operate from the Hôtel de Ville or the Mairie, but almost invariably they are both well-informed and helpful. It is as well to call in as soon as possible for any help or advice that may be useful. For instance, to collect a map of the town, obtain details of any forthcoming events, enquire about accommodation, the times of any special excursions, the availability of trains and buses and so on.

The relevant local tourist offices are listed in the Additional Information section at the end of each chapter.

Main French tourist offices are:

Australia
Kindersley House
33 Bligh Street
Sydney
NSW 2000
☎ (2) 231 5244

UK
French Government Tourist
   Office
178 Piccadilly
London W1V 0AL
☎ 071 491 7622

USA
610 Fifth Avenue Suite 222
New York NY 10020-2452
☎ 212 757 1683

Canada
1981 Avenue McGill College
Tour Esso Suite 490
Montreal
Quebec H3A 2W9
☎ 514 288 4264

Travel

By Sea
The way most people get to France from the UK is via a cross-Channel ferry or hovercraft. The shortest, cheapest and most popular of these is from Dover to Calais/Boulogne. On the Dover to Calais route you can usually get onto a ferry without booking, except for the most popular daytime or weekend crossings in midsummer. Even then, if you turn up at the port and the next boat is full, you should get onto the following one quite easily. The crossing only takes an hour and a quarter, and there are motorways or express roads both sides of the Channel to help you get to or from the ports quickly. Costs can be reduced by taking advantage of one of the special offers that the ferry companies make, or by the special discounts that some companies offer to shareholders. Most companies also operate a 'tariff' system, with cheaper tariffs for mid-week, night-time or out-of-season crossings.

The hovercraft crossings from Dover and Ramsgate to Boulogne and Calais are even quicker (35 minutes) but are more expensive, and space is more limited. Cars may be transported, but not caravans.

For anyone who enjoys a longer sea voyage Le Havre is almost as convenient.

By Air

There is no doubt that the quickest way of getting to France is by air. Strasbourg and Mulhouse both have international airports — the latter sharing this facility with Basel in Switzerland. Several other towns also have airports, such as Metz, Nancy and Colmar. Information about national and international flights is available from the offices of Air France.

By Rail

The two main lines serving the north-eastern region — one through Châlons-sur-Marne and Nancy and the other via Chaumont, Mulhouse and Colmar — eventually converge on Strasbourg. Motorail facilities are available to Strasbourg, Reims, Metz, Mulhouse and Nancy for people who wish to take their cars by rail. France has one of the most extensive railway networks in Europe with a variety of services and some special offers. These include things like holiday trains, coach excursions in conjunction with train journeys, rover-type tickets and specified reductions. It is worth making enquiries from the overseas offices of the French Railways to see exactly what is on offer.

Once in the area there are innumerable opportunities for exploring by train as even quite small centres have their own railway stations; added to which there is often a restaurant or a buffet attached where the food is good and not very expensive.

Rail Services

A number of services are offered by:
French Railways
Piccadilly
London W1V 0BA

Motorail
Information and bookings ☎ 071 409 3518
24-hour brochure hotline ☎ 071 499 1075

France Vacances Pass
Rail rover tickets for unlimited rail travel on any 4 days within 15, or any 9 days within 1 month, 1st or 2nd class.

These are available from: International Rail Centre, Victoria Station, London; ABTA travel agents; French Railways, London (personal application only).

By Road

Motorists who prefer to drive all the way by using the cross-channel ferries/tunnel can follow the *autoroute* from Calais to Reims or the *autoroute* from Le Havre to Reims via Paris. Thereafter the A4 *autoroute* carries on eastwards to Strasbourg with optional turnoffs in the Metz area southwards through Nancy or northwards into Luxembourg on the way to Belgium and Holland. There are plenty of opportunities for crossing into Germany, among them those at Saarbrücken, Strasbourg and Mulhouse, which also has an *autoroute* into Switzerland.

Preparing The Car

Before you set off, you need to be sure that the car is in good condition and fully equipped to meet French requirements. Have the car serviced before you go, and carry a few spares of essential small items like plugs, points, fan-belt, and a full set of light bulbs. As oil and distilled water are more expensive in France, you could carry a small supply of these too.

Two items you will need to meet French traffic regulations are: a red warning triangle, which you must place on the road 30m (98ft) behind your car if it breaks down and has no hazard warning lights (it is a good idea to use it anyway); and a headlight converter kit. This has the dual effect of adjusting your headlight beams for right-hand drive and changing the light to amber. A clip-on converter is the easiest way of doing this. You are required by law to adjust your headlamp beams and, though changing the colour to amber is not compulsory for tourist vehicles, it is advisable. It will make you more popular with French drivers, and you will not be constantly 'flashed' while driving at night.

You are required to carry with you the original of the vehicle's registration document, a full valid national driving licence and current insurance certificate. If the vehicle is not yours, you must have a letter from the owner authorising you to drive it. An national distinguishing sign (ie GB plate or sticker of black a white oval background) should be displayed near to late on the rear of the car, and on any caravan or ing.

Insurance

You should consider taking out three types of insurance: ordinary travel insurance to cover you for loss of possessions and money, and for medical expenses; special motor insurance to cover you for accidental damage to your car, and to other cars or people; and breakdown insurance, to give you extra protection against the expanse and inconvenience that can result from the car breaking down.

Personal Insurance

This is a good idea but not essential. Unfortunately there have been quite a few reports in recent years of cars being broken into and possessions taken, so insurance here is a wise precaution. Do not forget to report any incident to the local *Gendarmerie* straight away, or your insurance will not be valid. Keep any personal money with you at all times — do not leave it in your car.

Medical Insurance

Some medical insurance is now your entitlement under EC regulations — the same as that enjoyed by insured French nationals. You will need to obtain form E111, which you can do from your local post office. This will save you roughly four-fifths of your medical expenses, but to claim the other one-fifth you will need to take out additional personal medical insurance.

Motor Insurance

Ordinary UK motor insurance gives you only the legal minimum requirement for France. This is much less than the cover you would normally have at home, so although the Insurance Green Card (motor insurance certificate) is no longer a legal requirement, it is still important to provide this extra cover and to give evidence that you are fully insured. Get your Green Card from your car insurer well before you go. If you are towing a caravan or trailer, it should be endorsed for this at no extra cost.

Breakdown insurance can cover you for such things as freighting spare parts from Britain (spares for right-hand-drive cars may not be easy to find abroad); a hire car to continue your journey; or hotel costs while awaiting repairs. Some policies increase cover to stolen cars or to drivers who fall ill, but you are not normally covered for the cost of parts or for labour charges. These policies are usually called 'vehicle protection' or 'vehicle security', and are available from the AA, RAC, Europ Assistance, and the Caravan Club (to members only).

Though this type of insurance is useful if you have a major breakdown, are immobilised and need spare parts, it is not really necessary for minor problems, which can usually be solved by a local garage. Whether the insurance is worth the expense is for you to decide.

Accidents

One way to reduce the chances of an accident is not to drive too long without a rest. But if you do have one, you must inform the police, particularly if someone is injured. An accident statement form (*constat à l'aimable*) must be completed in all cases and signed by both parties (if appropriate). Any dispute should be taken to a local bailiff who will prepare a report, called a *constat d'huissier*.

Motoring Offences

On-the-spot fines are payable for a number of motoring offences including speeding and exceeding the drink driving level, payable in cash on the spot. The French have random breath testing and penalties are extremely severe. Therefore do not drink and drive.

If you do not consider that you are at fault, you will be asked to pay a deposit, or *amende forfaitaire*. This varies according to the offence you are charged with. The police must issue a receipt showing the amount paid.

Regulations

Apart from those mentioned above, there are some vital points about driving in France which you need to observe to avoid a hefty on-the-spot fine or worse. These are:

1. No driving on a provisional licence.
2. The minimum age to drive in France is 18
3. Seat belts must be worn by the driver and front and back-seat passengers.
4. Children under 10 years old may not travel in the front — unless the car has no back seat, or if the child is in a specially-approved back-facing seat.
5. You must stop completely at stop signs. Creeping slowly in first gear is not allowed.
6. No stopping on open roads unless the car is driven completely off the road.
7. No overtaking on the brow of a hill, where there is a solid single centre line, or where a 'no overtaking' sign is shown.

8. Use full or dipped headlights in poor visibility or at night. Use sidelights only when the car is stationary.

Rules Of The Road

In France you must drive on the right hand side of the road. You will be reminded by signs, at first in English as you leave Channel ports and later by the common and important sign *serrez à droite*. This means both 'keep to the right' and 'keep in the right-hand lane' on dual carriageways.

Another important road sign is *Priotitée à droite*. The rule in France is that, unless there is an indication to the contrary, traffic coming from the right always has priority. This applies particularly in built-up areas. The exceptions are either Stop or Give Way signs, where minor roads meet major roads. The sign *passage protégé* means that you are on a major road that has priority over side roads. On a major road, a tilted yellow square means that you have priority. One particular danger occurs at roundabouts — although the *prioritée à droite* regulation no longer applies here, many Frenchmen still drive as though it does. They **should** give way if you are on the roundabout and they are approaching but they may not! It pays to watch traffic coming from the right at all times.

Roads And Their Classification

French roads are classified A (*autoroute* or motorway), N (National road) and D (Departmental road). Signs for motorways are usually coloured in blue, while other roads are in green. Take care when approaching motorway entrance points: the signpost may indicate the same destination in the two colours, and to stay on the trunk road you must follow the green sign.

Most French motorways are toll roads or *Autoroutes à Péage*. They vary in price per kilometre, but they can be expensive, especially if you use them for long distances. They have emergency telephones, 24-hour fuel stations and *aires de repos* (rest places). These *aires de repos* are usually equipped with picnic facilities and toilets, and are sometimes attractively sited among trees.

You can find short stretches of motorway that are free. These are indicated on the Michelin maps with marker points and distance numbers coloured in blue rather than the normal orange.

The main trunk roads are National, with the number usually indicating the importance of the road. Thus single number roads

(N1 to N9) are usually wider and longer than double, which in turn are more major than three-figure roads. Single-number trunk roads are often almost as fast now as motorways; they are often dual-carriageway for long stretches, by-pass most towns, have restricted entry points and special services.

Departmental roads are often very good — well surfaced and maintained, and relatively traffic-free. They tend to vary in quality according to the prosperity of the department. They are usually narrower, but often better maintained, than three-figure or even sometimes two-figure N roads.

There is often confusion over the numbering of D and N Roads. The French Government, responsible for national roads, has handed over responsibility for many to the Departments, which has led to renumbering, so if you have an old map, the numbers may be out of date.

Speed Limits
These are lower in wet weather and low visibility than in dry conditions. In dry, unless otherwise posted, they are:

	Dry Conditions	Wet Conditions
Toll Motorways	130kmh (81mph)	110kmh (68mph)
Dual carriageways and non-toll motorways	110kmh (68mph)	100kmh (62mph)
Other roads	90kmh (56mph)	80kmh (50mph)
In towns	60kmh (37mph)	60kmh (37mph)

The limit starts with the town name, and the derestriction sign is the town name cancelled with a bar. The warning sign *rappel*, meaning 'slow down', means 'continue the restriction' when used in conjunction with a speed limit. There is a new minimum speed limit of 80kmh (50mph) for the outside lane of motorways, but only in daylight, on level ground and with good visibility. Drivers may not exceed 90kmh (56mph) for the first year after passing their test. Speeding offences may be fined on the spot.

Fuel And Garage Services
Essence, or fuel, comes as *ordinaire* (two-star), *super* (four-star), *sans plomb* or *vert* (lead-free), or *super sans plomb* (super lead-free). Unleaded fuel is widely available. Diesel fuel (*gazole* or *gas-oil*) is both widely available and much cheaper than normal fuel, the difference being considerably greater than in Britain. Vehicles equipped to run on LPG gas (Gepel/GPL) may be imported, and

many LPG filling stations can be found in France, especially on motorways. You can get a map showing their location free from LPG stations.

Most normal filling stations are now self-service, but someone should be available to *vérifier*, or check, the *huile, eau ou pneus* (oil, water or tyres), or to *nettoyer le pare-brise* (clean the windscreen). You are advised to tip for these services and you will usually have to pay for distilled water. Some garages make a small charge for air for tyres.

By Coach, Bus Or Taxi

There are very few long distance buses in France so visitors who want to travel by road, but are unable or unwilling to drive their own cars, or to hire one on arrival, should consult a reputable travel agent about the wide variety of coach tours that are available. These usually cover hotels and sightseeing as well and therefore people who want to be independent on arrival can make use of the local buses. They operate in large towns, in addition to which a great many small communities have their own local services. Details of these can be obtained from the appropriate tourist offices. There are also special excursions to places of interest, although these may only be available during the season. Taxis are plentiful and, obviously, more expensive than public transport. They have set charges but there may be instances when an extra sum will be added to the price shown on the meter, such as a drive with luggage to the airport. The cost of any long journey should always be agreed in advance and it is wise to get an estimate for a sightseeing trip round any large city.

By Boat

It is quite possible to travel by boat in north-eastern France, either by joining an organised cruise or hiring a canal boat with accommodation for two or more people. In the first instance the trip may be anything from a cruise down the Rhine to a pleasure steamer along one of the canals which operates a regular service lasting for an hour or two. In addition seats can be booked on a *bateau mouche* for a river trip in Champagne and also for excursions round some of the larger lakes.

A variety of boats can be hired in order to explore the canals. They are fully equipped for anything from 2 to 12 people and the prices include insurance, gas, bed linen and towels, technical assistance if necessary and vary according to the number of passengers and the time of year. Some addresses to contact are:

Chemins Nautiques d'Alsace
Port du Canal
F 67300 Schiltigheim
☎ (33) 88 81 39 39

Rive de France
Port de Plaisance
F57810 Lagarde
☎ (33) 87 86 65 01

Crown Blue Line
Le Grand Bassin
F11401 Castelnaudary
Cedex 01
☎ (33) 68 23 17 51

Car Or Bicycle Hire

If you go by air, fly-drive arrangements for hiring a car are available with the major airlines. Otherwise, you can make your own arrangements with one of the major car rental companies, which have offices in nearly all large towns. It is best to do this in advance from your own country. If it is more convenient, you can usually arrange to collect your car in one place and leave it in another, with no extra charge. To hire a car you must have a valid driving licence (held for at least one year) and your passport. The minimum age varies accordingly to the hiring firm but in general you have to be 21.

Central Booking Offices:

Avis
☎ (1) 46 09 92 12
Hertz
☎ (1) 47 88 51 51
Europcar
☎ (1) 30 43 82 82
Citer
☎ (1) 45 67 97 43

Thrifty
☎ (1) 46 56 08 75
Budget
☎ (1) 46 86 65 65
Mattei
☎ 91 79 90 10 or (1) 43 46 11 50
Eurorent
☎ (1) 45 67 82 17

Alternatively, you may consider it more healthy and close-to-nature to go by bicycle. Bicycle hire is widely available in France (ask at the local Office de Tourisme or Syndicat d'Initiative for details) or there are facilities at some 200 French railway stations. Some package holiday offer a combined travel and cycling-tour holiday in various parts of France. When hiring for yourself, you are advised to take out insurance before you leave.

INDEX

Page numbers in **bold** type indicate maps

MPC Visitor's Guides to
FRANCE

MPC Visitor's Guides to
FRANCE

Normandy Landing Beaches

Picardy & Pas-de-Calais*

Normandy

Paris

Champagne & Alsace-Lorraine

Brittany

The Loire

Burgundy & Beaujolais*

Vendée & Poitou-Charentes*

Dordogne

Massif Central

Alps & Jura

Aquitaine & Gascony*

Provence & Côte d'Azur

Languedoc-Roussillon & Andorra*

Corsica

Other Titles

Visitor's Guide FRANCE
For itineraries around the country, including Paris.

For a complete companion to Paris we recommend.
Paris Step by Step*

* Available 1995